D1233752

RC 607 .A26 H737 1988 26427Z

Holleran, Andrew.

Ground zero

FEB 1			
MAR 1			
MAY 11			
OCT 26			
MAY 23			

Missouri Western State College Library
St. Joseph, Missouri

GROUND
zero

Also by Andrew Holleran

Dancer from the Dance
Nights in Aruba

GROUND
zero

Andrew Holleran

Missouri Western State College
Hearnes Learning Resources Center
4525 Downs Drive
St. Joseph, Missouri 64507

William Morrow and Company, Inc.
New York

Copyright © 1988 by Andrew Holleran

All rights reserved. No part of this book may be
reproduced or utilized in any form or by any
means, electronic or mechanical, including
photocopying, recording or by any information
storage and retrieval system, without permission in
writing from the Publisher. Inquiries should be
addressed to Permissions Department, William
Morrow and Company, Inc., 105 Madison Ave.,
New York, N.Y. 10016.

Library of Congress Cataloging-in-Publication Data

Holleran, Andrew.
    Ground zero : essays / Andrew Holleran.
        p. cm.
    ISBN 0-688-07557-6
    1. AIDS (Disease)—Popular works.   2. Homosexuality, Male.
    I. Title.
RC607.A26H65   1988
306.7'662—dc19   88-2348
                                                                  CIP

Printed in the United States of America

First Edition

1 2 3 4 5 6 7 8 9 10

BOOK DESIGN BY ELLEN SASAHARA

Contents

8 Contents

"I have said that the soul is not more than the
  body,
And I have said that the body is not more than
  the soul,
And nothing, not God, is greater to one than
  one's self is,
And whoever walks a furlong without sympathy
  walks to his
    own funeral drest in his shroud . . ."

—WALT WHITMAN

"Terrors are turned upon me; they pursue my soul as the
wind; and my welfare passeth away as a cloud."

—THE BOOK OF JOB

Reading and Writing

TODAY THE GALLEYS of a book called *When Someone You Know Has AIDS* arrived. The book is addressed to two sorts of people: those with AIDS and those caring for people with AIDS. Since the line between these two categories is a thin and shifting one and merely the passage of time can put one on the other side of it, the book, like everything else about It, is something you grit your teeth to read, in order to prepare yourself for any new shocks. It would not be too much to suggest that much of a person's reaction to the subject of AIDS is directly related to his chances of getting it himself. Ask not for whom the bell tolls; it tolls for thee, citizen. If the man beside you at the lunch counter as you sip your soup can say vigorously, emphatically, "They should put them on an island and let 'em all die," that is because he has no fear of getting AIDS himself. The homosexual has no such option; he's part of it. What part he may not know. What part he may not want to know. But AIDS is not the only thing spread by a virus. Six years ago the media were so silent on the subject, gay men could not get *The New York Times* to even mention the fundraiser they held at Madison Square Garden to raise money for AIDS research. (The same weekend a march up Fifth Avenue in support of Israel was also ignored by the paper; the following week, deluged with protests from both groups, the *Times* apol-

ogized in print to only one—it was not the homosexuals.)
But now one can hardly pick up a newspaper or turn on
the television without confronting the subject. Most of us
have seen the statistics by now. Many of us have seen our
generation wiped out in announcements from the Harvard
School of Public Health. Some of us have been told we
were terminally ill by Barbara Walters. Which is why one
stops reading the stories finally, turns off the TV when
the topic is introduced, or closes the galleys of books like
the one that arrived this morning, wondering if—when
dying—you will think, *Oh,* this *was covered in chapter six!*
(As a friend said, "No one has to teach me how to die.")
As admirable as the writing or publishing of books about
AIDS may be, I really don't know who reads them with
pleasure—because I suspect there is one thing and one
thing only everyone wants to read, and that is the headline
CURE FOUND.

Someone at the Whitman-Walker Clinic in Washington
said that working with AIDS is like "staring at the sun"—
so, in a way, is even reading about it. When the plague,
or rather knowledge of the plague, appeared in New
York several years ago, I remember hosts telling guests
that they were not to talk about it at dinner. It spoiled the
party. A few years later I was so worried that the subject
would repel readers (I still assume this, since I, too, am a
reader and that is my reaction) that I discussed it only
when I had to; eventually, just as the dictatorial cruelty of
AIDS touched everything, it seemed I had to, all the time.
One reader accused me of exemplifying what a Jesuit instructor of his had called *morose delectation*—that is, the
cultivation of melancholy; the man who prodded an aching
tooth with his tongue rather than go to the dentist and get
it fixed. He was correct. But I didn't know where the dentist
was who could fix this. And though I relieved my own
anxiety and depression by writing about AIDS in these

essays ("Do you feel a *duty* to write about AIDS?" asked another friend), I turned myself, as a reader, to pure escape.

That first summer I picked up a novel of Henry James I'd not finished years ago: *The Golden Bowl.* It, too, was about death: the untimely death of someone young and fortunate. Then I read the life of Henry James himself, wondering how we had got from his sense of Victorian repression ("Live, live all you can, it's a mistake not to!") to our present predicament. But his biography could not explain the appalling news on CBS.

Journalists, said Schopenhauer, are professional alarmists, but if their news was needlessly plunging people into gloom (a man in Italy who confused his flu with symptoms of AIDS shot himself, his wife, and his child; a friend in New York took an overdose for the same reason), the facts seemed for a long while to justify their headlines. That was so because, from the start, fact has far outstripped fiction in this matter. Fact has been, like the virus itself, something individuals and society have had to struggle to catch up with, in a state of shock. Writers who dealt with homosexual life before the plague—the manners and mores of the homosexual community—have been quite left behind by a change of circumstances that blew the roof off the house they had been living and writing in. A novel about AIDS was written early on called *Facing It,* but that was just what I didn't want to do; at least in literary terms. Novels weren't needed; one only had to read the series of interviews carried in the *Washington Blade* with a man named Engebretsen, who allowed a reporter to visit him periodically as he withered away. The truth was quite enough; there was no need to make it up. To attempt to imagine such scenes seemed impertinence of the worst kind.

Meanwhile the *New York Post* began to shriek lurid headlines that in more innocent times many of us had collected as high camp: lovers jumping out of windows, hospital patients diving ten stories onto the sidewalk. The sexual practices of men who went to the Mineshaft were now known by married people who went home to Kew Gardens on the subway after a day spent working in Manhattan. Words and concepts previously thought too shocking to be mentioned came across the airwaves on National Public Radio, and I began to read books about other epochs in history when people had been subjected to cruel and unusual catastrophes. The Black Death was the most obvious; but when I looked at *The Decameron*, I saw the plague was merely the pretext for its storytellers to entertain each other with bawdy tales about ordinary life. So I turned to books on the French Revolution and the Terror (which is what most gay men in New York were going through at this time, exactly). The gouged eyeballs, footmen hacked to death in Marie Antoinette's bedchamber, beheadings in the Champs de Mars on guillotines that were, like AIDS, not always swift or instantaneous, seemed to match what we were being rapidly reintroduced to: the savagery of life. A savagery most Americans have always been spared. Then one evening I found an old issue of a *National Geographic* devoted to excavations at Herculaneum, the city destroyed along with Pompeii by the eruption of Vesuvius—and found the image I'd been searching for, in the skull of a woman with teeth clenched against the gas, pumice, ash suffocating her and her companions on a beach, as they tried to flee a city as helpless and startled and devastated as my own seemed to be. Disaster, real disaster, always comes as a shock.

A friend who was writing a novel on AIDS (it seemed inevitable there would be novels; indeed, most perversely of all, those being published that dealt with gay life, but did not deal with AIDS, were dismissed, reprimanded, for this fact) said he refused to write a "gloom and doom" book—but that was all there seemed to be around. Each time one tried to outline such a novel, one could not imagine the plot that would stand for, or include, all the stories one heard every day happening in reality to friends and their families in New York City and elsewhere—stories that broke the heart, if the heart was not anesthetized already. Writing about It, besides, presented an ethical dilemma: How could one write truthfully of the horror when part of one's audience was experiencing that horror? How to scare the uninfected without disheartening those who had everything to gain by cherishing as much hope and willpower as they could? "Don't you think it's time now," a friend said, "to introduce some light at the end of the tunnel?"

In those plays and films we had grown up with, of course it was, but when one sat down to think of some such illumination, there was nothing the *Times* had not done already in articles on AZT, or the galleys of the book that came today. Surely things had improved, in relative terms; one thinks still with pity of those friends who were the very first to get sick. Their dilemma and anger ("Why me?") were so awful; the first visit I made to a friend in the hospital convinced me, as I left his room, that the only moral thing to write now was comedy—anything to amuse, to distract, to bring a laugh, an escape from this dreary, relentless, surreal reality. But when it came time to make jokes, the air in which laughter thrives seemed to have dried up. How could one write comedy when the suffering was real? How could one write at all, in fact, when the only work that mattered was that of the men organizing social services, taking care of friends, trying to find a microbiological solution to a microbiological horror in laboratories we could not see? When World War I began, even Henry James abandoned fiction altogether—that huge edifice of prose, that elaborate manor house of tales and metaphors

—and went to London to visit soldiers back from the front. (As had Whitman during the Civil War.)

And just as James realized that novels were beside the point, or were at least momentarily repudiated by the fantastic brutality of war, so now the act of writing seemed of no help whatsoever, for a simple reason: Writing could not produce a cure. That was all that mattered and all that anyone wanted. One couldn't, therefore, write about It— and yet one couldn't not. A vast sense of impotence—the same helplessness the doctors were beginning to feel— spread over everything. The only conceivable function of writing about It seemed to be to relieve the writer's own anxiety and depression; but who needed that? The *Times* was now running virtually an article a day about some aspect of the plague: its effect on the arts, its effect on doctors, its effect on fashion, its effect, even, on the Pines. Films made for television, plays, and short stories began to appear. Publishers wanted a novel. The novel is occasionally the way we bring some sort of order to the disorder of life. But *this* disorder seemed way beyond the writer's powers. Literature could not heal or explain this catastrophe; the one thing about the plague that became clearer as it progressed was its senseless, accidental, capricious quality. This dumb virus killing the thing it fed on, destroying an organism infinitely more complex, advanced, skillful, *human* than it: Was there a lesson to be learned? Yes. That we live on a planet in which many forms of life still feed on each other. Beyond that—despite the vast "I told you so" of the Bible readers—there was nothing else to say. Not about homosexual life, certainly. If the homosexual life-style that had evolved before the plague was good or bad, contributed or did not contribute, to human happiness, that was an issue to be addressed on its merits or lack of them. No one had led it, after all, in the light of the plague. No one expected it to charge that sort of price. The wider the field the plague moved across, the more unrelated its targets—nuns, babies, African heterosexuals, American homosexuals—the more meaningless it became. The plague may well turn out to be an irrelevance, an aberration, an interruption in the flow of history—a kind of fatal flu that had no more moral or metaphorical or social significance than the common cold. World War I, we say, had causes, meanings, lessons. The Spanish influenza, which carried off hundreds of thousands after the war, did not.

And yet because as long as it lasts, we must think of it as a war and not some fatal flu, writing about AIDS will appear, and in the short term will almost inevitably be judged, I suspect, as writing published in wartime is: by its effect on the people fighting. Indeed, it must be about fighting—it must be in some way heartening—it must improve morale, for it to be allowed a place of honor. Otherwise it will be dismissed as useless, discouraging, immoral, like any art that accepts surrender during a war; even though the plague has in reality produced a deep depression—a depression that alternates between numbness and horror, fatigue and fear. For a certain segment of the American population, the plague has been a cram course in death.

For this very reason friends argue that gay life has come of age in dealing with all this suffering, that gay men and their relationships with one another have been changed forever. But I wonder. What is there to learn? A great many people lived a certain life that, within the bounds of what they knew at the time, was reasonably safe. But, like schoolchildren who learn years later that the school they attended was lined with asbestos; or like families who are told, twenty years after buying a house, that they live on a mountain of PCBs, the homosexuals who lived in New York, San Francisco, Los Angeles in the seventies, lived with a devotion to health and appearance that was part of their stereotype, learned afterward that all the while there was an invisible germ circulating in the fluids of their sexual partners that was capable of entering the body; of lying undiscovered, unnoticed, unseen for several years; and then of destroying the system of biological defenses by which humans have been able, through years of evolution, to live on the planet. This plague was retroactive—and hence it seemed doubly meaningless, doubly unfair. It was so unfair that it simply belonged to that category of events —earthquakes, droughts, tidal waves, volcanic eruptions— that simply happen and that engender in those who survive nothing more than a reminder of how unstable a planet this is. Someday writing about this plague may be read with pleasure, by people for whom it is a distant catastrophe, but I suspect the best writing will be nothing more, nor less, than a lament: "We are as wanton flies to the gods; they kill us for their sport." The only other possible enduring thing would be a simple list of names—of those who behaved well, and those who behaved badly, during a trying time.

Ground Zero

THE METROPOLITAN THEATRE—though one never used the second word, so that when you told someone where you were going, it might have been the Museum or the Opera—is no longer as dark as it used to be. The two long hallways running down either side of the ground floor are brightly lighted now, and the foyer downstairs is actually visible. In the seventies the darkness of the Metropolitan was legendary; to walk into this decrepit theater on Fourteenth Street and Second Avenue was to enter a deep black cave in which it was impossible to see anything—that was the point—but now, in March 1987, the strictures of safer sex have resulted, even here, in brighter light bulbs, and the place seems small.

Much about New York seems small to me now, however—as if the whole city has shrunk to a single fact. I wander around the city, past the buildings going up on Third Avenue, the crowds on Fifth, aware that inside the external aggrandizement of the city's power and glitter is another, smaller city that haunts the mind as a sort of doppelgänger. The city as cemetery. When I come home to New York now, I go straight to one of the movie houses showing pornographic films near my apartment on the Lower East Side. At the end of a day spent visiting friends in hospital rooms, intelligent, brave, accomplished men breathing oxygen through tubes, staring at a brick wall

19

outside the window, when I get down to the street, my instinct is to run, not walk, straight through this earthly hell to the Metropolitan and, once its doors close behind me, relax; relax in the comfort of the very thing that has become the Siamese twin of death. After leaving the hospital room of the friend whose pancreas has ceased to function, after leaving the apartment of the young man going blind, after meeting on the sidewalk a thirty-six-year-old acquaintance who looks eighty-nine, I walk through the cold, crowded city or down a deserted street to one of these doorways and obliterate everything in the dark, warm chamber of seed. Nothing else provides the comfort this place does—no other experience.

There is something sad, delicious, and infinitely erotic about these movie houses now that in the past seemed merely sordid. The Metropolitan has always been here—it still even costs the same three dollars—but it depressed me in the seventies; I must have gone there two times the entire decade. Often I walked by it. Passing the Metropolitan, I always thought of a story by Tennessee Williams called "The Mysteries of the Joy Rio," about a dirty old man in the balcony of a dirty old movie house. The Metropolitan was synonymous with sleaze—famous for mixing a clientele that consisted of successful models from the Upper East Side with residents of the Lower East Side; one of those places where two groups that did not meet often socially could meet in the dark. It was so dark one could hardly see any of the men lining the hallways, the balconies, the stage behind the movie screen—and all I remember now is the feeling one had standing in the lobby, buttoning one's coat, before going back out onto the street: that dull, depressed feeling of failure, of dejection—at having to rejoin a world in which light, law, manners, reality kept one at a distance from the objects of one's erotic dreams. Sometimes I would walk afterward across Union

Square to a bathhouse that only cost three dollars, too. But now the baths are closed. Despite the fact that they are a sensible environment for the practice of safe sex, the Hassidim picketed the one on my block, the courts acted, and its black doors are shut. A few remain—on Wall Street, in Harlem—but they don't seem worth the trouble; in middle age, one prefers what is closer to home. And the Metropolitan is a five-block walk from my apartment, one block farther than the Jewel.

My urge to run here immediately upon returning to New York is fueled by not very mysterious things—the reasons people go to these places in ordinary times: loneliness and lust. But it's also a response to the fact that New York is no longer a city one returns to anymore with the exhilaration and joy that used to make one consider kneeling down on the airport tarmac, like the pope, and kissing the ground upon arrival at Newark. New York is the center of the epidemic, where you learn almost inevitably that another friend is sick or see those who already are, knowing all the while you cannot do anything but behave as well as possible and wonder if they hate you for not being there with them. Depression is what brings me to the pornographic movie house—the same way it sent me home from the hospital the autumn I spent visiting a relative in Intensive Care (among the nurses, tubes, machinery and horror), to turn the TV on to *Mister Rogers' Neighborhood,* because he was so soothing, simple, and calm. There is an urge, when life seems totally crushing, to just crawl back into the womb.

And the womb is what these theaters—the Metropolitan, the Adonis, the Jewel—seem to me now: dark and quiet and calm. They are, moreover, all that is left, it seems, of homosexuality. Or at least one aspect of it: the central one. "I don't know anyone who's gay anymore," says a woman I know. "Gay is not an option." The bars, the discotheques,

that are still open seem pointless in a way; the social contract, the assumptions, that gave them their meaning is
gone. They turn you serious, if you stay long enough—
because every bar, every dance floor, reminds you eventually of a friend. The memory of friends is everywhere.
It pervades the city. Buildings, skylines, corners, have holes
in them—gaps: missing persons. And if the present is a
cemetery, the future is a minefield. I think sometimes that
if, in the old days, over a long enough period of time,
everyone had slept with everyone else, one might now say,
"Over a long enough period of time, everyone is diagnosed." The pitier becomes the pitied eventually. As one
man said after being diagnosed, "I wasn't doing anything
everyone else wasn't." Exactly.

Years ago, when the first friend died, those he'd left
behind talked about his illness for months; the whole city
seemed haunted by him; we could not imagine New York
without Eddie. Now when the news comes that the twenty-
fifth or thirty-ninth friend has died, I discuss the death,
and before hanging up the phone, ask the person who
brings these tidings if he wants to go to the movies Tuesday. It's nearly banal. Won't someone please turn off the
bubble machine? We get the point. The friend who lives
upstate says calling friends in Manhattan is "like phoning
Germany in the thirties." Or, as a friend who lives in town
puts it, "It's like living in Beirut. You never know where
the next bomb is going to go off." The bomb seems the
best metaphor as I wander the Metropolitan. "Oh," people
say when they learn someone left New York in 1983, "you
got out before the bomb fell." Well, not really, he wants
to reply, the bomb fell several years before that. Only we
didn't know it. The bomb fell without anyone's knowing
the bomb had fallen, which is how it destroyed a community that now seems—looking back—as extinct as the
Mayans.

The Mayans left temples in the Yucatán; we seem to have left pornography. At the Jewel—around the corner —they show films in which the actors are all men; the first time I went there I sat for hours watching them, the way one might watch a movie about Chichén Itzá. It seemed —this sunny Californian world that provided our sexual icons—as distant from the present as life upon the pyramids of ancient Yucatán, divided from the present—in both cases—by a single cataclysmic fact. People go to the Jewel not only to watch the films, however. They go to cruise, to breathe the forbidden atmosphere. What persists through all this is the allure of the body. "The skin," a man at the Jewel explained, when we left together in a cab, "needs to be touched." (His apartment, on the other hand, was littered with three-by-five cards on which he'd written, BHAGWAN, PLEASE PROTECT ME FROM AIDS. We ended up talking, not touching—the exchange of stories, of fear, that sometimes replaces sex itself.)

At the Metropolitan—for a reason I never understood fully—the mostly gay audience watches (or does not watch) heterosexual fantasies on-screen. That is part of the mystique, the legend, of the Metropolitan—the illusion that this place was more *real.* Now things are too real, of course, and the Metropolitan seems fantastic. The women in black lingerie, garters, and stockings produce a cascade of fervid gasps, an "Oh! Oh! Oooooh!" in the backseat of automobiles, a tent overlooking Big Sur, a train compartment, that makes one think men do not even come close to enjoying sex, that only women experience pleasure. The men attending them on-screen seem merely drones—as nervous, and harried as bank robbers pulling off a job. The men in the audience sit for the most part alone—straight men, perhaps, who don't care what the rest of the audience is doing, or men whose egos require that they establish their masculinity by watching women first, or simply men who need the time to adjust their eyesight to the darkness and to figure out just what is going on and who is here.

Who is here are mostly black and Hispanic men. The graffiti in the hallway reads, among other things, STOP NIGGERS FROM SPREADING AIDS and PUERTO RICANS RULE. Fifty-three percent of the cases in New York City are now Hispanic and black (which has more to do with drugs than with homosexuality and more to do—most cruelly—with babies than with right or wrong). For a while, blacks thought it was a white man's disease, and whites thought blacks had caused it: Africa accusing Europe, and Europe accusing Africa. Everyone wants someone else to have AIDS, if someone has to have it. Farther down the wall in the same handwriting are the words EVEN A SIMPLE BLOW JOB CAN GIVE YOU AIDS. USE RUBBERS AND LIVE! (Most gay men do not believe this; they think oral sex is safe.) Rubbers are something one was once embarrassed to even suggest—at the beginning—for fear one would be considered anal-compulsive, neurotic, germophobic. Rubbers were jokes, the idea of constraints on sex anathema to those who argued that the essence of sex was freedom, and the glory of freedom sex. "He said he'd use a rubber," one friend told me, "if I'd eat what was in it afterward." Safety ran counter to the whole expansive spirit of the seventies, the exhilarating suspicion that we were pioneers in the pursuit of human happiness and no one had found its limits yet. The plague provided limits. Limits that seemed so draconian and harsh that even after their arrival—during that period when people knew, but did not quite believe—friends considered infringements on their sexual options to be merely more American puritanism. There was no romance in rational sex. (The curious paradox of anonymous sex, of one-night stands, of places like the Metropolitan, was their deeply romantic nature.) The death of Dionysus— the closing down of promiscuity—took a long time to complete itself, a lot of fear. But fear was what the plague has produced copiously, till it now constitutes the substance of homosexual life. AIDS has been a massive form of aversion therapy. For if you finally equate sex with death, you don't have to worry about observing safe-sex techniques; sex itself will eventually become unappetizing. And the male body will turn into an object of dread—not joy—an object whose touch makes you lie awake afterward, with the suspicion you have just thrown your life away for a bit of pleasure. "There's so much more to life than sex," says a friend who has sworn off it for several years now. "What?" I say. "Well, living," he says. "Living is important to life." Yet despite this—because of this—we come to the Metropolitan.

I come to the Metropolitan for the same reason friends began traveling to Brazil when the plague began—escape. But standing there letting my eyes adjust to the darkness I cannot help but think of friends who are not there with me—seeing what I see. Life's a movie people leave at different times; the ones who remain get to see a little more of what happens next. Eddie and I used to see things together—now I come here alone. "I'm going to Ceil's for lunch, then the D and D Building, then down to your neighborhood for a Shiatsu massage from that Dutch boy, and then I thought I'd drop by the Metropolitan," he'd call and say, reciting a menu for the afternoon that only a city like New York can offer. "I'll wait for you before going in. It's only three dollars!" It was much more expensive than that—but we didn't know this when we met on the sidewalk in a lightly falling snow that dusted the mustaches of the young Puerto Ricans passing the glass doors of the theater that separated the public from the private world. Eddie usually wore his torn fatigues and ripped tank top, under an Armani topcoat. His motto was Auntie Mame's: "Life's a banquet, and most poor fools are starving to death." Eddie's not here now. Other people are. They wander back and forth—across the foyer, up and down the aisles, searching, searching.

Sometimes we forget how far we've come, or at least how much we have assimilated, in the past four years. The shock is gone now, perhaps, the dangers accommodated in daily life. Each person makes his daily wager with the facts. The telephone still strikes a residual fear each time it rings—it will bring, for sure, more bad news—but it's not what it used to be: the panic of a shark attack. Yet the sadism, the cruelty, the meanness of the disease, remain the same. It may no longer surprise but it still takes the breath away—and makes you yearn for an end to the suffering. "I keep thinking there's a beach at the end of this," a friend said. "An island, and we'll be happy again." In the meantime, I come to the Metropolitan the moment I get back to Fun City.

And it is fun—the old freedom, the old romance, the old excitement, come back the moment the doors to the lobby close behind me, and, after allowing my eyes to adjust to the darkness, I start to walk around. There may be far fewer vignettes—people have adapted; they always do—but there are still some. Two men squat downstairs on toilets in the bathroom stalls, cans of beer lined up in a row at their feet, peeking out around the partitions to see who's coming, with the expression of children waiting for Santa Claus. When the plague began, and I heard stories of people with AIDS having sex with others without telling them till it was over, I thought them preposterous; now, given the depression, the despair, the idea that what-the-world-gave, I-can-give-back, I believe them all. The prostitutes with AIDS who keep going back to work exemplify a strain in everyone. The best guide to this mysterious battleground in which death may be entirely hidden was given by a friend with AIDS: "Treat everyone as if they have it." Caveat emptor. That really is all people need. No legislation is necessary. The Metropolitan seems so dangerous that it's safe. When I go upstairs again, I notice that most men watching the movie sit alone in their seats—alone and safe—but others are walking back and forth along the dark rear walls that lead up to the balconies. Even there, at the darkest center of the Metropolitan, the men leaning against the wall of the projection booth are separate. No clumps, no orgies; none of the feeding frenzies that, even before the plague, made one wonder what it all meant. In the darkest corner, the handsomest Puerto Rican in the place—so far—is being licked by someone I cannot see. Next, a handsome youth who looks as if he just got off the bus from Indiana comes up the stairs, can of beer in hand; his bright eyes, broad-shouldered frame, wide-open expression (what does it mean?) are the image of health, the look cereal companies use in commercials. He walks onto the narrow balcony, sits down next to a black man who is leaning against the wall, and stares at him . . . the white man watching the black man, the black man watching the white woman on the screen . . . till the black man approaches his seat and there is a connection: like a car stopping at a gas tank, a bee on an azalea in spring. The mouth fits over the tube, the figures merge in silhouette, and a crowd gathers to watch what many of them will not do themselves anymore.

For if the plague is now part of everyone's information kit, the individual bargains people make with it are just that: entirely individual. Someday—not just yet—there will be novels about all of this, but they will face the problem writing about it stumbles against now: how to include the individual stories, the astonishingly various ways in which people have behaved. Downstairs, at the end of the hallway that runs the length of the theater, brightly lighted now, a handsome Puerto Rican stands before a man kneeling in a shadowy curve in the wall. As I watch, the Puerto Rican removes his penis from his pants and slaps it against the palm of his hand. It's a form of theater. When the man on his knees hobbles over to approach the penis, the Puerto Rican says, "No!" and glares at his supplicant, who then backs up and begins to masturbate, till the man on his knees in the corner ejaculates onto the floor. It lies there, like plutonium. "Thanks," he says, getting up. "You did this just right. You were terrific." He zips up his pants and adds: "Do you want a condom?" A token of thanks the Puerto Rican accepts from his admirer, who then leans against the door and falls out onto the street—the final testimony to this performance the fact that he can leave now, he has got what he came for, and needed. Ah, New York: always the same, ever new.

Snobs At Sea: 1983

SOMEWHERE IN *Remembrance of Things Past*—which is to say, for the reader unable to find the line, somewhere in Russia, or the Amazon—the shock of learning that a rich man has fallen in love with a prostitute is compared to the trouble we have believing a man can die of a common bacillus. It's a complex metaphor—comparing the course of love with the course of disease (Proust's favorite link), and social snobbery with the biological superiority human beings feel to other forms of life. The idea that an intelligent man with aristocratic friends, a fortune, family, career, can fall for a kept woman—or, in our day, be converted to a jar of ashes on the bookshelf by the action of an organism invisible to the naked eye— is somehow very hard for us to grasp. "The germs don't need me," said a friend at the baths one evening when I asked him if he wasn't worried about dying. "If they needed me, I'd be worried, but they don't need me."

In his metaphor the germs are hostesses making up guest lists for dinner parties, I guess—yet "The germs don't need me" is perhaps only the craziest version of a denial that a lot of us have practiced over the last two years, even while the people we have played with over the last decade and a half keep disappearing. We haven't, really, somehow, believed in this germ. However, the last line of a letter tells me as an afterthought that the weather of March 29 in

New York was snow and sleet: "Perfect for Ray's funeral." I did not know Ray was sick, much less dead. This evening I am told on the telephone that Michael won't live past the weekend; CMV virus is running riot through his system, he is bleeding internally. But Michael went to *Cornell*, I think when I put down the phone; came from a good family; has a little garden on East Seventh Street he was always asking me to come see; was someone I have always had a crush on. What did the germs need with him?

He was, after all, a talented architect who had come to New York after college to work and enjoy himself—a modest agenda in the scheme of things. We met because I liked his roommate—a scientist with Bell Labs who took a class in gymnastics I attended at the West Side Y. Our first outing ended with my being dropped off in a taxicab at my corner, while Michael, in the backseat, smiled a knowing grin as I bid his roommate good-night—as if Michael knew exactly what had, or had not happened; as if he were saying, "This one isn't what you think he is." Or, "You got no further than any of the others who've tried." His roommate eventually grew tired of the commute from Manhattan to southern New Jersey and vanished from the city. Michael stayed. The striking thing about Michael—the first time we went home together—was that, in contrast to his roommate, he was easy. Very easy. So easy that the fact that our attempts at sex failed in no way affected the affection we felt for each other. Michael was good-natured. Had a good sense of humor. And was less sexually inhibited than most people.

This was not, in the seventies, something that lowered him in my estimation—nor any of the other friends I had who went out searching for whatever we were searching for with a determination approaching dementia. Sex was partly what we had come to New York for, from families, universities, small towns, other cities. I'd come upon Michael summer nights with his lover, floating down a near-empty Broadway on bicycles; they spoke of moving to a farm in upstate New York, or Georgia, but never seemed to manage to. I would see him instead on the beach at Fire Island. Or on the sidewalk in front of my apartment, buying flowers, on his way home from work. Or in a room at the Saint Marks Baths. The last time I'd seen him at the baths, in fact, I'd walked into his room before I realized the body was his; and then, in a split second of recognition, two steps from his pillow, we both laughed. It was a compliment, in a way—freed of the formalities of friendship, stripped of his social identity, and clothes, Michael was so desirable I'd taken the risk of stepping through the door. That door, of course, had been open to anyone who passed; there was something concupiscent, lascivious about Michael. The sheets he lay on were rumpled and damp with use, the light bulb by the doorway red, the skin of his body shining with a film of oil. This greasy red chamber of love that eventually ended up as part of the towering heap of garbage, on the sidewalk outside the Saint Marks Baths was something he made jokes about when I met him in a suit and tie there the next day, coming home from work; black plastic bags filled with the detritus of lovemaking, cans of Crisco, lubricant, poppers, paper plates, cups, packs of cigarettes; the whole effluvia of a disposable culture that had decided to dispose of sex the same way the Japanese restaurant a few doors down got rid of its grease.

Time magazine called it a sexual revolution (which it then declared *finito* in March 1984). Whatever it was—the pent-up frustration of lonely years in high school; the delayed release of urges that had been a source of anxiety and fear since puberty; or just the mating instinct in a new context, Michael exemplified its inexhaustible energy. He had first fallen in love with a professor at Cornell—a married man who left his wife for him and then went back to her—and

I imagined Michael searching ever since in the baths for some recapitulation of this youthful love affair. No doubt that was romantic. But in a way the whole phenomenon was. I pictured a line of Yeats's chiseled above the doorway of the public clinic on Ninth Avenue where Michael and I went to have our stools analyzed, our blood tested. "Love has pitched its mansion in the place of excrement." Curious location. But then whatever one came down with could be cured. If we were playing on a garbage dump—that heap of black plastic bags on the sidewalk Monday mornings on Saint Marks Place—it was under control. Penicillin had made sex possible, the way plastic paved the way for swimming pools and airplane seats. It made accessible to the average man a dream of sexual paradise previously confined to the canvases of Delacroix, the pages of *The Arabian Nights*. When we saw the red tea tent of an Indian moghul at the Metropolitan Museum in the India exhibit, it reminded Michael of the billowing pavilions people set up on Fire Island: a silken dream of Eros.

It was just that connection between art and life, history and the present, civilization and Eros, that Michael appreciated—his favorite things were art and sex. Paintings, sculpture, architecture—and bodies. One hot afternoon when the beach on Fire Island was closed to swimmers because the sewage our Baghdad dumped off the coast had drifted dangerously close to land, Michael and I talked for a while beside the sweltering sea. All around us the crowd of men broiled in the sun, beside an ocean they could not enter. Unreal sea! It looked in fact perfectly beautiful, immense, invigorating—so green I stood skeptically at the edges for almost an hour before I saw the first tiny fleck of raw sewage, like a jellyfish in a transparent wave, floating into shore. Only then did I give up thoughts of swimming and go back. There was no way to know this day—all of us marching up and down beside the polluted sea—was the future. "There's nothing worse than an ocean you can't swim in," Michael said as we returned to town on the nearly empty train. "Unless it's people you can't sleep with," he added with a smile. "I guess that's why the baths are so . . . relaxing."

Years before, a man had told me in a restaurant on Fifty-seventh Street that a doctor he knew was predicting a tremendous epidemic of typhus in the gay community—but it seemed at the time, over chicken-salad sandwiches, just an instance of an ancient paranoia, a biblical vision of punishment-for-sex. No one *I* knew had typhus. Nor did I know that eventually not the outer but the inner ocean would turn foul: the sea of fluids that composed us. Little did we dream, nights at the Saint, when sweat was licked off dancers' bodies and kisses were exchanged, that years later we would refuse to drink from the water fountain there. It took a while for people to believe in the invisible—the germ—for the same reason it took the nineteenth century a while to accept Pasteur's explanation of smallpox; but once accepted, the implications were mind-boggling.

It was thought when this began that those exposed to the virus—"infected" was somehow too harsh a word at the time—were simply the very reckless; the extraordinarily debauched. Then, as the numbers mounted, it seemed they were not very different from you and me. And the next popular hypothesis arose: Everyone had met these germs, but only some would succumb. (People were not ready to believe you could catch cancer the way you caught hepatitis.) When Michael got sick, he would stop and talk outside the baths on my block on his way home from work, and save for the fact that he no longer went in himself, he seemed perfectly normal. His illness did not upset me because its effects were not visible. He even seemed to be recovering under the care of a nutritionist. The only change

I could see was that he seemed to wear a coat and tie more often—and he discussed his T-cell count, the results of his latest blood test. He was the example I reserved in my mind to prove it could be beaten, or at least lived with; it was not this fatal, fantastic, unbelievable thing it seemed to be. Eddie was going up to Sloan-Kettering every other day for the most avant-garde and technological of treatments, ever ready to try the new and the sophisticated. Michael, on the other hand, credited a macrobiotic diet with bringing his T-cell count back to normal (for a homosexual, that is; there were three categories, he told me with an ironic smile: Virgin, Average Man, and Homosexual). We laughed at this odd reminder that being the third, we were not the first two. He had his setbacks. One evening on his way to one of those Christmas parties New Yorkers give that, we agreed, are sometimes pointless and fatiguing, he was tired before even getting there; he'd just recovered from a bad day and was still angry that his lover had not brought him the soup he'd asked for, when he could not get out of bed. His life was quieter now, but by no means over; in fact, his work—his career as an architect—prospered. He no longer went to the baths or Fire Island. He went to Rome instead that spring and, on his return, began to paint the ceiling of his apartment with a fresco found in a church or palace there—an admirable whimsy, it seemed to me, like Michael himself, like art these days, half-jest, half-glory. He seemed, in short, to have changed his habits—which consisted now of work, macrobiotic diet, and sitting in the garden he kept inviting me over to see, the garden I wanted to, meant to, see but did not because it was just a few blocks away and I would surely see it some evening.

Instead we sat on the stoop across from the baths on my block—which continued to draw men from all over the city and country—and watched people go in and out. "They want to commit suicide," said Michael. "In a few months they'll all be sitting in a doctor's office." The people at the baths said, "All life is risk." Homosexual men were either Puritan or Cavalier, and it all depended on your attitude toward something we could not see.

Before Michael died, I sometimes went into the baths and sat at the counter of the little restaurant to see the men going by the doorway in their towels—the baths, after all, were supremely visual—and sometimes, having seen a certain man. go by the doorway in his towel, checked in myself and hung around the hallways in the darkness for a couple of hours, watching people I had not seen in some time, people who reminded me of the men you ran into at the Everard in 1971—and not only reminded me; some of them were.

They were as improbable and beautiful lying in their rooms in their Jockey shorts and towels as the gods Michael had painted on his ceiling on Seventh Street—a burst of beauty, fantasy, art—in the midst of a nightmare reality. The thrill of homosexuality is finally an aesthetic thrill. They lay there exactly as I wanted them to; not so much gods floating on celestial clouds as river deities, lying on the shore of some sacred stream between the mud and the bulrushes. Dark, gritty, salubrious mud. "Life is risk," one said, "I don't care if I die tomorrow." Or: "The germs don't need me." And: "You can't stop living." But of course you can. It still seems against nature, a violation of the hierarchy of things, that a microbe could destroy a man who could stop on a summer evening and talk about friends, Rome, Christmas, while the city he loved went past us. It still seems a scandal that an item scientists do not even define as living—a microbe that can't paint angels, trumpets, clouds, or gods upon a ceiling—can devour a creature who can. It still seems a reproach that a virus can return us from the twentieth century to the Stone Age. Yet that is the revolution this thing has effected; that is the toppling that has occurred—the world turned upside down. Human beings lie broken and shattered on the ground, like statues pulled down by barbarians invading Rome, or Protestants smashing the art in a cathedral. The basilica's empty. The church is closed. Michael—who went to Cornell—is gone. And sometime this summer, some ignorant tenant will move into that apartment, unpack his bags, kill the first cockroach, lie down to rest, and find himself staring in surprise at a host of gods and goddesses, angels bearing trumpets, golden clouds—all painted by a man the germs needed, for what I do not know.

Bedside Manners

"THERE IS NO DIFFERENCE between men so profound," wrote Scott Fitzgerald, "as that between the sick and the well."

There are many thoughts that fill someone's head as he walks across town on a warm July afternoon to visit a friend confined to a hospital room—and that is one of them. Another occurs to you as you wait for the light to change and watch the handsome young basketball players playing on the public court behind a chicken wire fence: Health is everywhere. The world has a surreal quality to it when you are on your way to the hospital to visit someone you care for who is seriously ill: Everyone in it, walking down the sidewalk, driving by in cars, rushing about on a basketball court with sweat-stained chests, exhausted faces, and wide eyes, seems to you extremely peculiar. They are peculiar because they are free: walking under their own power, nicely dressed, sometimes beautiful. Beauty does not lose its allure under the spell of grief. The hospital visitor still notices the smooth chests of the athletes in their cotton shorts as they leap to recover the basketball after it bounces off the rim. But everything seems strangely quiet—speechless—as if you were watching a movie on television with the sound turned off, as if everyone else in the world but you is totally unaware of something: that the act of walking across York Avenue under one's own power is essentially miraculous.

Every time he enters a hospital, the visitor enters with two simultaneous thoughts: He hates hospitals, and only people working in them lead serious lives. Everything else is selfish. Entering a hospital he always thinks, *I should work for a year as a nurse, an aide, a volunteer helping people, coming to terms with disease and death.* This feeling will pass the moment he leaves the hospital. In reality the visitor hopes his fear and depression are not evident on his face as he walks down the gleaming, silent hall from the elevator to his friend's room. He is trying hard to stay calm.

The door of the room the receptionist downstairs has told the visitor his friend is in is closed—and on it are taped four signs that are not on any of the other doors and are headlined, WARNING. The visitor stops as much to read them as to allow his heartbeat to subside before going in. He knows—from the accounts of friends who have already visited—he must don a robe, gloves, mask, and even a plastic cap. He is not sure if the door is closed because his friend is asleep inside or because the door to this room is always kept closed. So he pushes it open a crack and peers in. His friend is turned on his side, a white mound of bed linen, apparently sleeping.

The visitor is immensely relieved. He goes down the hall and asks a nurse if he may leave the *Life* magazine he brought for his friend and writes a note to him saying he was here. Then he leaves the hospital and walks west through the summer twilight as if swimming through an enchanted lagoon. The next day—once more crossing town—he is in that surreal mood, under a blue sky decorated with a few photogenic, puffy white clouds, certain that no one else knows . . . knows he or she is absurdly, preposterously, incalculably fortunate to be walking on the street. He feels once again that either the sound has been turned off or some other element (his ego, perhaps with all its anger, ambition, jealousy) has been removed from the world. The basketball players are different youths today but just as much worth pausing to look at. He enters the hospital one block east more calmly this time and requests to see his friend—who is allowed only two visitors at a time, and visits lasting no more than ten minutes. He goes upstairs, peeks around the door, and sees his friend utterly awake. The visitor's heart races as he steps back and puts on the gloves, mask, cap, and robe he has been told his friends all look so comical in. He smiles because he hopes the photograph that made him bring the copy of *Life* to the hospital—Russian women leaning against a wall in Leningrad in bikinis and winter coats, taking the sun on a February day—has amused his friend as much as it tickled him.

"Richard?" the visitor says as he opens the door and peeks in. His friend blinks at him. Two plastic tubes are fixed in his nostrils bringing him oxygen. His face is emaciated and gaunt, his hair longer, softer in appearance, wisps rising above his head. But the one feature the visitor cannot get over are his friend's eyes. His eyes are black, huge, and furious. Perhaps because his face is gaunt or perhaps because they really are larger than usual, they seem the only thing alive in his face; as if his whole being were distilled and concentrated, poured, drained, into his eyes. They are shining, alarmed, and—there is no other word—furious. He looks altogether like an angry baby— or an angry old man—or an angry bald eagle.

And just as the hospital visitor is absorbing the shock of these livid eyes, the sick man says in a furious whisper, "Why did you bring me that dreadful magazine? I hate *Life* magazine! With that stupid picture! I wasn't amused! I wasn't amused at all! You should never have brought that dreck into this room!"

The visitor is momentarily speechless: It is the first time

in their friendship of ten years that anything abusive or insulting has ever been said; it is as astonishing as the gaunt face in which two huge black eyes burn and shine. But he sits down and recovers his breath and apologizes. The visitor thinks, *He's angry because I haven't visited him till now. He's angry that he's here at all, that he's sick.* And they begin to talk. They talk of the hospital food (which he hates too), of the impending visit of his mother (whose arrival he dreads), of the drug he is taking (which is experimental), and of the other visitors he has had. The patient asks the visitor to pick up a towel at the base of the bed and give it to him. The visitor complies. The patient places it across his forehead—and the visitor, who, like most people, is unsure what to say in this situation, stifles the question he wants to ask, *Why do you have a towel on your forehead?* The patient finally says, "Don't you think I look like Mother Theresa?" And the visitor realizes his friend has made a joke—as he did years ago in their house on Fire Island: doing drag with bedspreads, pillow cases, towels, whatever was at hand. The visitor does not smile—he is so unprepared for a joke in these circumstances—but he realizes, with relief, he is forgiven. He realizes what people who visit the sick often learn: It is the patient who puts the visitor at ease. In a few moments his ten minutes are up. He rises and says, "I don't want to tire you." He goes to the door and once beyond it he turns and looks back. His friend says to him, "I'm proud of you for coming."

"Oh—!" the visitor says and shakes his head. "Proud of *me* for coming!" he tells a friend later that evening, after he has stripped off his gown and mask and gone home, through the unreal city of people in perfect health. "Proud of me! Can you imagine! To say that to me, to make *me* feel good! When he's the one in bed!" The truth is he is proud of himself the next time he visits his friend, for he is one of those people who looks away when a nurse takes a blood test and finds respirators frightening. He is like almost everyone—everyone except these extraordinary people who work in hospitals, he thinks, as he walks into the building. The second visit is easier, partly because it is the second, and partly because the patient is better—the drug has worked.

But he cannot forget the sight of those dark, angry eyes and the plastic tubes and emaciated visage—and as he goes home that evening, he knows there is a place whose existence he was not aware of before: the foyer of death. It is a place many of us will see at least once in our lives. Because modern medicine fights for patients who a century ago would have died without its intervention, it has created an odd place between life and death. One no longer steps into Charon's boat to be ferried across the River Styx—ill people are now detained, with one foot in the boat and the other still on shore. It is a place where mercy looks exactly like cruelty to the average visitor. It is a place that one leaves, if one is only a visitor, with the conviction that ordinary life is utterly miraculous, so that, going home from the hospital on the subway, one is filled with things one cannot express to the crowd that walks up out of the station or throngs the street of the block where he lives. But if the people caught in the revolving door between health and death could speak, would they not say—as Patrick Cowley reportedly did as he watched the men dancing to his music while he was fatally ill, "Look at those stupid queens. Don't they *know?*" Guard your health. It is all you have. It is the thin line that stands between you and hell. It is your miraculous possession. Do nothing to threaten it. Treat each other with kindness. Comfort your suffering friends. Help one another. Revere life. Do not throw it away for the momentous pleasures of lust, or even the obliteration of loneliness.

Many homosexuals wonder how they will die: where,

with whom. Auden went back to Oxford, Santayana to the Blue Nuns in Rome. We are not all so lucky. Some men afflicted with AIDS returned to die in their family's home. Others have died with friends. Some have died bitterly and repudiated the homosexual friends who came to see them; others have counted on these people. Volunteers from the Gay Men's Health Crisis have cooked, cleaned, shopped, visited, taken care of people they did not even know until they decided to help. One thing is sure—we are learning how to help one another. We are discovering the strength and goodness of people we knew only in discotheques or as faces on Fire Island. We are following a great moral precept by visiting the sick. We are once again learning the awful truth Robert Penn Warren wrote years ago: "Only through the suffering of the innocent is the brotherhood of man confirmed." The most profound difference between men may well be that between the sick and the well, but compassionate people try to reach across the chasm and bridge it. The hospital visitor who conquers his own fear of something facing us all takes the first step on a journey that others less fearful than he have already traveled much further on: They are combining eros and agape as they rally round their stricken friends. As for the courage and dignity and sense of humor of those who are sick, these are beyond praise, and one hesitates where words are so flimsy. As for a disease whose latency period is measured in years, not months, there is no telling which side of the line dividing the sick and the well each of us will be on before this affliction is conquered. We may disdain the hysteria of policemen and firemen who call for masks, and people who ask if it is safe to ride the subway, and television crews who will not interview AIDS patients. For they are not at risk—those who are, are fearlessly helping their own. This is the greatest story of the plague.

Cleaning My Bedroom

IT'S A TYPICAL East Village apartment —if there is such a thing: ceilings of average height, a big kitchen, a front room (which is really in the back of the building), short hallway with bathroom, and bedroom. The bedroom gets no light, and looks out at a brick wall about two feet away. It was the first apartment I had without a tub in the kitchen, however, and therefore has always seemed to me luxurious. When I moved in, I got all my furniture from the street—chairs with busted springs, et cetera— built shelves out of concrete blocks, and bookcases of metal milk crates. The paint was peeling off the walls and ceiling, there were roaches in the kitchen, the window in the bathroom was broken, and the bedroom dark—but it all worked, because it went with the neighborhood, and neither it nor I had any pretentions in matters of decor. The Frenchman I invited over one evening understood when he walked in: "Ah," he said, as he looked around, "*la vie bohème*." Friends called it the Tomb of Ligeia.

That's all it was for several years—until the roommate I acquired one year decided, the winter I was gone, to renovate the kitchen and the room he slept in. He hired a young carpenter-designer who transformed the two rooms into gleaming white simulacra of the photos published in *The New York Times*'s home section: sanded floors, Formica counters and cabinets, dimmers and ceiling-high bookcase.

The detritus of the renovation was put in my bedroom: two-by-fours, plaster, discarded molding, manuscripts (in large extra-strength trash bags), lamps and blenders, vegetable juicer, silverware, ceramic chotchkas for the kitchen no one ever used or threw out, bookends, phone books, phone table, headdresses worn to the Feather Ball, thrown in a heap in the back room. The carpenter who did the work never took down the old timbers and bags of plaster—the apartment is on the sixth floor—and when I returned, after the renovations were complete, and peeked around the bedroom door (which now opened only a crack), I was astonished by the proportions of the rubble. It seemed, curiously, to represent my own collapsed life in New York at that time: I was hardly there anymore, and since I never used the room for anything but sleep, and my roommate never used it at all, it seemed reasonable that it should remain a garbage dump. The timbers I took down, because nails were sticking out of them—and a few bags of plaster (though the bedroom ceiling periodically supplied more) —but I left everything else. Everything else was covered with dust, a fine gray-white dust: the towel hanging on a nail in the door, the green trash bags filled with manuscripts, the books on the windowsill, the windowsill, the suits and shirts hanging from a pole at the end of the room. The sheets were mercifully covered with a comforter, though once I returned to find a dark stain of urine and heap of hardened cat turds on that: The cat, driven mad by a full litter box, had shat on my bed, using the room as her place of refuge, too. Even this did not compel me to clean the place out, however. I aired the comforter over the windowsill in the front room, shook the dust out of my towel, and continued my vacation. My vacations—those biannual visits to New York lasting a week or two—were so important to me I did not think it worth my time to clear the bedroom. I was only there to sleep, change clothes, use the phone.

Of course a bedroom is in fact used for much more than that—it's the temple of our psyches, the place in which we can shut out the world, make love, read, unwind, daydream, sleep, lie abed Sunday morning with the newspaper, close the door on the whole stressful, high-strung life that begins the moment you leave your house or apartment. It's a New Yorker's chief retreat; the place of last resort; the Cave of Somnus, the River of Lethe, the Temple of Eros. Once my bedroom had been a kind of shrine to which I brought back human gods—found, like my furniture, on the street (O wondrous city!). I would, like a good altar boy, light the candles, some fat, some thin, which lined the windowsill on glass saucers, to view that most holy object (the body) in their light. On such evenings— the door shut, the candles burning with still, upright flames in the windless air, the radiator pipe hissing, a man in bed beside me—this room was the most enchanted place in the world, or at least the very reason I lived in New York.

Now those days are past; one day years ago my roommate and I agreed not to bring people back to the apartment for sex, out of deference to each other; the plague began; and the candles that had illumined these sacred, paradisical, sometimes comic, sometimes depressing moments, are now covered with dust themselves and sit unused, guttered, waxy, gnarled, on glass saucers so encrusted with ash and soot they seem made of another material. And I come home to bed now with merely the newspaper and an ice cream sandwich, to unplug the phone, stash it among the garbage bags, read the next day's headlines, and then turn off the light, falling asleep finally on mountains of junk—mountains of junk that, I realize now, made me feel as temporary, as uprooted, as depressed as most of the people I know in New York these past four years: afraid of the future, horrified by the present, not knowing what to think of the past.

And now that the sky itself seemed to have fallen in upon us, the plaster dust and shards, the heaps of unused objects that I climbed over to get to my bed, or the pole on which my shirts hung (embroidered now with ermine collars of dust) seemed perfectly true, right, appropriate, in tune with the times. The young man who did the renovation recently decided he loathed homosexuals and homosexual life, and no longer even speaks to my roommate when they pass on the street. My roommate's new friends, in turn, have nothing to do with his milieu in the seventies (gym, Saint, Fire Island); and his new life—macrocrobiotics, celibacy—seems to turn its back on the past with an almost surgical finality: like Harriet Craig, he keeps his countertops, pots, and pans scrupulously clean in the new kitchen. Only the bathroom and short hall leading to my refuse-heaped bedroom remain in the premodern state. My roommate showers at his new gym, far, far from Sheridan Square, and does not use the bathroom much; it and the crummy hall outside seem to form a buffer zone, a transition period between his devotion to a New Age and my remaining in the Past.

The Past has exploded in our face like some car on a streetcorner in Lebanon. When I went out the door one morning to spend a day on Fire Island, he looked at me and cracked, "Don't be wistful!" But wistful was exactly how I planned to feel. When I found one afternoon a trove of photographs my roommate had taken during summers at the beach, I sat down and pored over them. They seemed at first as innocent as all photographs of summers at the beach: men lying on blankets under a cloudless blue Atlantic sky. The men were all muscular—so muscular their bodies seemed to have nothing to do with their much smaller heads. The handsomest was now dead. He lay on the blanket with four other men, bound together by some invisible witticism, their bodies curled with a laugh about to explode from their lips. The longer I looked—at the silver-sharp sunlight, the wide beach, the distant and irrecoverable laughter—the more extraordinary he seemed: free, stylish, burnished by the sun; paragon of a way of life whose main sense of proportion had to do with muscle groups. But that was thought for some other time; on their face, the photos were so delightful, I put them on the kitchen table with a note for my roommate to find.

When I returned that evening and asked excitedly if he had seen the pictures, he looked across the two chopsticks suspending a strand of boiled seaweed at his lips and said, "I threw them out." "Why?" I asked. "Because I don't want to look at dead people," he said. "That's morbid." I did not say that was no reason to consign them to the trash— but that was his reaction to the horror; mine was to pick the packets of photos out of the garbage can and put them back in the bedroom, where they would presumably remain intact, in my Museum of the Past.

I had been removed from New York in 1982 through circumstances that had nothing to do with the plague— but now when I returned to Manhattan for those brief visits, I felt like the World War II veteran who returns home a stranger to his wife and children. The cat recognized me—I think—but my roommate did not; he told me which pots and pans I was to avoid (like kosher implements, reserved for macrobiotic cooking) and even left a frosty note one morning after he'd gone to work about my use of a forbidden frying pan the night before. All these things hurt. But his friends were dying; my friends were dying; and New York was merely a place where one went to funerals and avoided the eyes of other men on the street—at least, in our generation. The things on which we based our lives had proved disastrous. The rubble in my bedroom was no less than the rubble of our friendship, the rubble of homosexual life, the rubble of fear, the uncertainty, the impossible present and grimmer future. The cosmic transportation system must be very busy, a friend now living in San Francisco wrote one evening; there are so many trains taking away the dead; while reading the obituaries in the *Bay Area Reporter* in a restaurant on Haight Street, he burst into tears. Another writes at three in the morning from Seattle, because he is awake with diarrhea, about a new infection his doctor has just told him he has. I climb over the shards of plaster, dust, trash bags of failed novels, to reach my toothbrush, towel, and finally bed, and relax only when I shut the light off and plunge the whole room—like the letters, the place, the headlines of the *New York Post* about a man I know with AIDS jumping out the window of his apartment with his lover—into darkness.

It is not that life in New York has ended—young men walk down Saint Marks Place at six o'clock on their way home from work with perfect haircuts and dreams as romantic as mine when I arrived in town. Friends still take shares in houses on Fire Island and give a party for their new housemates, and watching them—good-looking, giddy, hopeful—I am reminded that in this vast and various city, in the midst of the plague (or New Age, depending on your viewpoint), everything still goes on, somewhere. My roommate wants to forget everything about the Past; others I meet stop me, like the Ancient Mariner, to reminisce, starry-eyed, about people, parties, an era so free of care it seems to them mythical. And why not? We want the past five years to be a nightmare one wakes up from; we want it all to have been a bad dream and not something we will have to live, or die, with for the rest of our lives, like the fallout from Chernobyl. We want there to be a whistle, or siren, that signals "All Clear." Fear and hope come and go in alternating waves, prompted by the latest statistic, phone call, newscast, blood test. Conversations that begin on the old high note end in gloom. The homosexual world—its common language—is broken up now. There are many dialects. Many conditions—some sick, some well, some with reason to worry, others with none. It's as eclectic as life in New York: In any crowd walking down Saint Marks Place, young men in business suits carrying attaché cases, skinheads with great prongs of hair radiating from their scalps, fifties haircuts on Elvis Presley profiles, boys who want to look like Japanese art students in Paris, men with the long hair and pony tails I last saw in the sixties, and—a small fraction of what used to be the cutting edge—museum-quality clones in mustaches and jeans. The city is all jumbled up. The ghetto has blurred, unraveled, like the sexuality of individual gay men. Friends of mine, turning homophobic, say they're attracted only to straight men or women; when they look at homosexuals, they think of death. The Saint—that cathedral of the seventies—is now desanctified; friends who went there with religious fervor now go to a Sufi dance class. I cannot tell who is gay or straight in the East Village, and when I go to the bars, one has no sense of the mood of the man across the room. It is probably like yours: bedeviled, frustrated, and cautious. Yet at the Palladium you can still dance to "Golden Oldies"—the cream of disco from the seventies—in a nest of Puerto Ricans in muscle shirts and dark glasses who are obviously drugged. The floor is jammed with gym bodies. But when "Love's Theme" comes on, and I look up to remember the dead friend who loved this song ("Listen to the violins going up, up, up!" he used to say), a huge volleyball net descends from the ceiling and an enormous balloon, which the dancers hit back and forth across it. So much for remembrance. So much for trying to draw a line between the past and the present. There is no clear boundary between the two. Though I may ask myself, *What would X be doing today if he were alive?* and, *How would gay life have evolved had there been no plague?*, the answers would be meaningless. He's not, and there was, and that's that. And these reflections somehow—over the course of a night's sleep—produce the next morning, when I awaken, a decision to clean my bedroom.

It is one of those tasks you do by not stopping to plan —by saying aloud, "Don't think about it. Just start with that pile." The papers I touch send up clouds of dust that make me sneeze, the heaps look insurmountable, but I go ahead because I want, for the first time in four years, to walk on the floor. I have not walked on the floor in four years because I've been intimidated by the proportions of this rubble, but now I pick up all the dusty, dirty clothes and take them to the laundry on Second Avenue; then excavate the rest—jackets, sweaters, bathing suits, parkas, boots, sweatshirts, jeans, books, letters, bank statements, travel brochures, schedules of ferries to Fire Island, Long Island Railroad timetables to Sayville and Freeport, a pool schedule for the McBurney YMCA, two tennis rackets, an old passport, a cash machine credit card that is no good, old running shoes stiff with dust, pornographic magazines, a collage of photographs I'd composed on a piece of cardboard linking nude men I thought belonged together, an invitation, stamped on a coaster, to a Wild West party at the River Club—the archeological evidence of a life that seems to have been unable to locate a golden mean between Trivia and Catastrophe. Then I find my journal. The journal—when I open it and choose an entry at random —reminds me again of the friend I thought of the previous night on hearing that song by Barry White and the Love Unlimited Orchestra. On 5/22/74:

"The Island: Running along the beach in the Pines from Water Island, the sun on the sea, that feeling—sitting by the pool with T. after ham sandwich and beer—carpenters hammering all around—Rosa stoned in the bushouse, getting packed, singing, 'My man loves my big dick, and the bigger it gets the more he likes it.' "

The first person is alive; the second is dead, but he lives again, completely, in that bawdy song. The other entries reflect the same dichotomy. I read a few more descriptions: of sex partners, trips to San Francisco, Fire Island; and then put it aside for the moment, caked with dust, open a drawer and pick up several guest passes to a gym I no longer belong to; a dusty slide of a man I thought the handsomest on Fire Island in the early seventies; a tube of Bain de Soleil 6 (we now prefer 15; the sun is considered as lethal as sperm); a checkbook I thought I'd lost; the metallic ruler with which I measured my penis after I moved to New York and learned that these dimensions mattered; bottles of moisturizer; a squash racket with a broken string; Rilke's *Letters to a Young Poet;* Freud's *Civilization and Its Discontents;* an invitation to an exhibit of a friend's architectural drawings, from August 20 to September 15, 1983, at a gallery in Southampton. (Can George be dead only two years? It seems much longer.) In the same heap of papers the invitation is in, I find a plastic sandwich bag in which two white Quaaludes and a shattered, pale blue Valium lie. Quaaludes: Relaxation of the sphincter, the langorous erotic surrender forbidden now. What would I do if I took these Quaaludes now—yoga? I put them in a drawer, pick up a scrap of paper, which I read and try to make sense of: *Michael Greenberg, Sweeney Todd (tire store), Christopher Street.* What does that mean? My bedroom is half cleared, and I put the scraps in a basket on the chest of drawers, sexual confetti, in a wicker Out box. Then I pick up the old issue of *Honcho* (April 1979). Inside is a long article on fisting by James Henry—celebratory, informative, upbeat. A doctor is interviewed. The author closes with a recollection of one of his "best experiences ever. Two lovers, both into fisting, both with magnificent, talented holes. We did a threesome on an outdoor waterbed on Fire Island, in the middle of the afternoon." He speculates about the future: "It is possible, given our sophistication and jadedness, that such an esoteric practice . . . will someday be the norm for homosexual men. . . . Or perhaps sexual heads, and the trips that go along with them, are subject to change and evolution." (You bet.)

"We may all wind up back in a heavily oral stage . . . we may wind up tripping out on ourselves in elaborate multimedia jerk-off trips. Others say we'll be into asexuality." (How prescient!)

"Who knows? Whether fisting is here to stay, or just the hit of the seventies, I'm glad I'll be able to tell my hypothetical grandchildren what it was like when fisting was young." *When fisting was young*—it seems, this jaunty piece, like a letter written by someone in the lounge of the Titanic: "Having a wonderful crossing, the food is superb, Father and I are just about to go down to dinner." (Crash.)

Circles

I MET COSMO his first year at the university in Philadelphia, my first in law school—our friendship was rooted in a time and place I considered idyllic even then. Life consisted simply of books and sports and long, clear twilights waiting for night to fall so one could go to the bars. I lived in a highrise for graduate students a block from a brand-new gymnasium with an Olympic-sized pool and beautiful new squash courts. Cosmo lived a few blocks away in an apartment off-campus, with a friend who was a dancer. The dancer was a bit snotty. Cosmo I liked from the start. He was a gymnast, and though gymnasts (and dancers) are, I often think, somewhat cold, he was not; he was reserved, poised, organized, but he was very good-hearted. He was small, but perfectly formed, in face and body; had Cosmo been tall, he would have been breathtaking. As it was, he was quite something. We both loved the gym. The gyms at that university were two: one small and brand-new, the other cavernous and nineteenth-century. In the old gym, men swam naked in the marble pool, and the locker room had a ceiling so high it was like a train station, and in the dim, gray air one would see athletes standing at the bottom of diagonal shafts of light as they removed their clothes, transfixed, like nudes in Thomas Eakins. The gymnasts had a huge room upstairs. Cosmo spent hours there, but I was afraid at first even to enter it. I had come to sports late in life, disliking them as a child, knowing, in my heart of hearts, as the baseball descended from the sky toward the ineffectual glove I held outstretched in my pessimistic hand, that I would not catch the ball, was not suited for baseball or the company of other boys. And years later I still had to overcome a great deal of fear and self-consciousness to enter a locker room and use the facilities of a gym, as if at any moment someone would recognize me as an imposter. But at a large university, in an enormous gym, self-consciousness dissipates. You are on your own. No team is going to groan when you miss the ball, and no parent is in the stands watching you play. You are left alone in a huge, sunny room, on a golden, polished floor, with a pair of chalk-whitened rings suspended in space, inviting you to try a muscle-up. That's where I met Cosmo.

Cosmo was the best at tumbling and mat exercises—back flips, handstands; but he was also expert enough on the stationary rings, and pommel horse, and parallel bars, to teach me those. My goal was a handstand on the rings and circles on the pommel horse. Cosmo was a patient teacher: cool, calm, humorous. Though he was far beyond my beginner's level in the sport he pursued with the thoroughness of a perfectionist, he was always willing to help. He seemed from the moment I met him master of things I wanted to learn. In fact, Cosmo awed me slightly, because, while six years younger than I, he seemed several years more poised. He was one of those people who strikes you, even in school, as knowing what they want. I did not. I would often leave the books on contracts and torts unread on my desk to go down to the gym in the middle of the afternoon and try hanging from the rings, balancing on the pommel horse, perfecting my handstand. Destiny—in that somnolent world of gyms and libraries—seemed more bound up with my body than my mind, though the guilt

this engendered only increased an air of apology Cosmo
was quick to make fun of. He had, besides a mania I did
not share for puns, a somewhat wicked sense of humor.
Cosmo was not his real name. In high school, his classmates had nicknamed him Cosmopolitan; I think they must
have been responding to that quality which Cosmo had
even before I met him: a certain self-possession. He came
from a large Midwestern city he expressed no particular
desire to go back to. He seemed, on his ten-speed with his
knapsack, utterly independent, as if all he needed in life
was a combination lock, a Penguin paperback, and a can
of V-8 juice. Even greater proof in my mind of his sterling
character was his complete disinterest in the bars downtown, which, like gyms, I had only recently discovered and
could not get enough of. He did like to go to the beach,
however, and the two of us went to Atlantic City together
Atlantic City in 1970 was divinely seedy, in a physical,
not moral, sense: crumbling, faded, forgotten; a ram-
shackle, salt-misted facade of huge hotels with grandilo-
quent European names (the Marlborough-Blenheim, the
Chalfonte, Haddon Hall), overlooking a brown beach and
even browner surf. We were happy there—those long afternoons when the men hawking ice-cream sandwiches
stomped about the hot sand in boots with thick soles and
two pairs of cotton socks. Cosmo and I would lie on our
blanket, talking in British accents, mine that of a BBC
announcer, his that of a Cockney prostitute. Why I don't
know. But all Cosmo had to do was blare some cheap
sentiment in the voice of that British tart to crack me up
—perhaps because Cosmo himself was so well-mannered
an example of WASP reserve. In everything else (including
the sensible manner in which he brought in his knapsack
lotion, water, oranges, a Penguin paperback on Hinduism,
extra money, clean T-shirt, hat), he was the soul of reason.
So that when a momentary confusion about what to do

with his life occurred that year, it did not surprise me when he resolved it quickly by deciding to study architecture. About the same time I left law school because I could no longer endure torts, Cosmo was accepted by Columbia, and when he moved to New York to study, I moved to New York to move to New York.

He praised the Columbia gym on the telephone; I joined a course in gymnastics at the West Side Y. From time to time I saw Cosmo downtown, including one morning on Avenue A when he introduced me to his new lover: a man who seemed to me a worthy catch—handsome, smart, a sense of humor as dry, if not as wacky, as Cosmo's. He was also an architect, and when Cosmo graduated, he went downtown to work and live with him. The lover disliked sand. So Cosmo and I went to the beach together—first to Fire Island and then to Jones Beach because it seemed more convenient in the end. The lover was anxious and ambitious for the firm he had founded, and during those early lean years, I felt guilty calling on Cosmo. When I went to pick him up at the loft he shared with John, I felt slightly sub-rosa, like a nine-year-old playmate who calls on a friend to take him out to do something naughty. Yet we were doing nothing so awful. All we did was what we'd done in Atlantic City: talk in British accents, laugh, and lie on our blanket discussing the bodies passing.

Cosmo admired the male body, and so did I: I was even more addicted to bars, beaches, and gyms than I'd been in Philadelphia. About the time I moved to the McBurney Y on Twenty-third Street, Cosmo joined the Sixty-third Street Y to work out with the gymnastics squad there. His body was always a shock to me when I saw it on the beach—without the wristbands, chalk whitening his hands, the worn gym shorts and T-shirt, the wire attached to a belt which enabled him to learn a dismount from the rings without falling. His body—hardened to a fine edge through hours and hours of the painstaking repetition of certain moves that, unless they are done perfectly, do not count at all—was, like that of a ballet dancer, so tight, so chiseled, it seemed out of place against the blowsy, lazy, limitless stretch of soft sand, heaving sea. Yet Cosmo knew how to unwind: remove a banana from his knapsack, peel and eat it as if it were quite something else before turning to his suntan lotion. The contents of his knapsack never changed, nor did the contents of our friendship ("Would you do my back?"), which was why it meant so much to me: Cosmo was a link with the academic world I'd left behind in Philadelphia. He stood for all the things I still, at bottom, loved more than any others: books, wit, the body, a beach in summer, a friend to laugh with and sit beside on the train going back to the city—tired, spent, completely happy— as the big red sun winked between the buildings of Queens.

There was also something else about him, something morally solid, that I admired. One day when I mentioned my confusion about whether a blind person in public wants assistance or not, Cosmo said, "Just go up and ask them." He had an uncle who was blind. That Cosmo knew this etiquette did not surprise me, nor did the fact that his business finally prospered. I was proud when an apartment Cosmo and John had done was "published" in the *Times*. In fact, because Cosmo and John were witty, smart, good-looking, I always wanted to invite them to parties, introduce them to friends—but I never did. For one thing, they had no need of friends; they had each other. They wanted to meet clients, I suspected, and that was that. So I would, on my way home from the Y on Twenty-third Street (where I eventually moved) merely ring their buzzer and go upstairs to talk. We always had fun, and on one occasion Cosmo lent me a book he liked: *The Philosophy of Andy Warhol, From A to B and Back Again*.

It was not a book I particularly wanted to read—the one

area in which I perhaps did have confidence was reading—
but for some reason that evening I let him press it on me,
thinking that if Cosmo found it special, I should check it
out. It was another connection between us (just as friends
who constantly borrow money from each other are, I sometimes think, only asking for proofs of affection). In fact it
only confirmed my disinclination to borrow books. I read
just a few pages and then put it beside my bed on the
humidifier. People who borrow books, or money, or anything else, I've always felt, are under an obligation to return them as soon as possible; but I let Cosmo's loan gather
dust beside my bed for quite some time because I thought
I must be wrong about the book and intended to give it
another chance. After all, Cosmo had recommended it.

In the meantime, as in some fairy tale, the years passed
happily. I was published, Cosmo prospered, and we acquired what, when still in school, one fears one never will:
a vocation and a source of income. We saw each other at
the gym, or at the beach, riding back to town after those
perfectly happy afternoons, with our knapsacks, sunburns,
as the sun loomed very large and red beyond the dirt-
encrusted windows and Cosmo—by merely widening his
eyes over someone's conduct in the next row—broke me
up. I forgot about the book; I forgot about the humidifier,
an item which, when I bought it, had been touted as the
magic means to moist skin and, months later, been exposed
as the means by which bacteria circulate through a room.
We were very health-conscious. So much for trends. Life
proved as reversible as the function of the humidifier. The
decade of—among other things—meeting Cosmo at Jones
Beach, the baths, his loft, ended abruptly in 1981 when I
was forced to leave Manhattan for family reasons.

For the next four years, I did not see Cosmo; when I
came back to the city on visits of one or two weeks, I walked

by his loft overlooking Madison Square and looked up at the window and at the rings hanging from his ceiling. I thought often of pressing the buzzer and just dropping in. Just dropping in on friends as one walks around New York is one of its great pleasures, but it's tricky, in a way: One doesn't want to drop in at the wrong time, or drop in and not be welcome. And the truth was I always called Cosmo; he never called me. So I'd sit for a while on a bench in Madison Square and look up at the window instead. During the years I was mostly out of New York, during the years his book lay beneath bags of manuscripts and plaster and dirty clothes, during the years I did not really know where I lived, and felt that I belonged neither to New York nor to the cities I was in, I did not have the sort of ebullience one needs to drop in on people you don't see often. People were dying, people were changing, and stopping by to visit a friend meant talking not about the baths, the beach, the gym, but death. So I would merely think of ringing the bell; that's all; then leave town without doing it. Instead I sent Cosmo from Cleveland one fall a clipping about a house there (because he grew up in Cleveland), and he sent me back a clipping about a project of his own in Manhattan, which struck that note of professional pride that made me feel I did not have that much in common with Cosmo any more. For if youth lies on a beach discussing men with no thought of the morrow, middle age shrinks life to Career.

Then one spring I returned to New York in a different mood: The changes that had been so painful seemed complete; people seemed to have constructed sane lives around the plague. When I did visit friends, we did not talk about It with the same leaden finality at the end of every conversation. I even began to think that the worst was over and that those alive were the lucky survivors. And one

April afternoon, I cleaned my bedroom—the physical expression of a mental change—and came upon the book Cosmo lent me nearly four years before.

It was clear to me now I wasn't going to read this book, and since I'd had it quite long enough, I decided that returning it was the perfect pretext to see Cosmo. But I did not rush to the phone. Why not? Because the four years that had passed since I'd seen Cosmo were not just any years; they were a sort of minefield. Then one day a friend got me into the McBurney Y, and not only did I recall, instantly, how for years in New York the gym was a source of pleasure, but I found myself growing mentally more confident about everything. And one afternoon I returned from a swim at the Y in so buoyant a mood my fears seemed simply silly. And I picked up the phone with only one worry: that I'd get the new scourge of New York—the answering machine.

Instead, I got a human voice, a gentle, smooth, resonant voice—typical of Cosmo and his crowd, in a way: calm, friendly, intelligent. I asked if Cosmo was there. "Cosmo?" he said. "Cosmo?" And I heard a shuffling of objects, a pause, as if he were looking around in embarrassment. Instantly, I thought, *Cosmo and John have split up. This is the new lover. The replacement.* Then he asked who was calling; I said I was an old friend. He said, "Cosmo died." Now, even the reception of bad news is accompanied by a thrill, a frisson—when a macabre premonition is fulfilled; and yet as I stood there trying to absorb this juxtaposition of subject and verb, discounting all the factors that pollute grief with vanity, and noting I half suspected the news and was attracted, meanwhile, to the voice of the man on the phone who told me, even after reminding myself that everyone must die sometime, that there have been plagues in human history before, that our emotions really do not amount to much in the vast scheme of the universe, that

billions of people have died before this and billions will
after, there was still something about this two-word sentence. Each question I fired at the gentle voice on the
phone was only an attempt to dilute the shock, by acquiring
concrete details. I asked how, when, how long. For there
seem to be two ways people die of AIDS: slow and fast.
Cosmo was fast. Two weeks. No symptoms, pneumonia,
boom. And part of what I was feeling was terror—since
each time a friend dies of this thing, your own hunch that
you will escape seems less and less rational. And part of
this sadness was that I had no one to mourn with; none
of my friends knew Cosmo; he was not part of my circle;
he belonged to those sleepy days in Philadelphia that seemed
so innocent now. I had no one to tell the news to, and thus
relieve the sting. I asked how Cosmo's lover had taken it;
the voice explained that he could never have spoken this
way had John not been out of the office at that moment.
But John was getting better. I said, "Do you still get calls
like this, asking for Cosmo?" and he replied, "Not as often."
I thanked him and hung up, and wandered into the next
room with the words *Cosmo died* repeating in my mind,
thinking Cosmo was not like everyone else. Cosmo was
special. Sure, everyone is special in one sense; in another,
everyone is not. I sat down at the table and stared at the
Times I was reading before I made the call—the headlines
describing the nuclear accident at Chernobyl, the radio-
active cloud drifting across Europe, the story in section B
that said that by the year 2000 New York City could be 60
percent Hispanic, black, and Asian American. In other
words, the world, and the city, would go on evolving, de-
veloping, without Cosmo. And I sat there for some time
until I decided, later that evening, to go back to the gym,
as if in motion, exertion, the cool, athletic use of the body,
I would let this shock dilute itself.

Downstairs the weather had changed; after a warm couple of April weeks—Cosmo had died in September—it was nippy again, like a fall night. The World Trade Towers twinkled in the blue dusk. The crowds surged down Saint Marks Place. There was an enormous NYU dormitory going up on Third Avenue. The city was booming. Yet a small part, an individual cell, of Manhattan had been extinguished. Out of the huge honeycomb of the city I walked through, one chamber was empty. Okay. By now we are so accustomed to obituaries, they have become a literary genre—and the fact is, the thirtieth death of a friend does not shock you as much as the first did. While much may be behind us (the initial shock, confusion, blame, numbness), one thing is not—everything may be over but the dying. That will go on. Even so, Cosmo's death horrified. What a waste! What an insult! Having heard so many theories by which people explain what is still the inexplicable (why some die, others do not), I could only think they were utterly inapplicable to this one. I didn't think his death fit any theory, or moral judgment, or pop-psychological hypothesis (that those who die hate themselves, or are emotionally blocked, or unable to love, or ashamed of being homosexual—or any of the other current placebos circulating with increasing seriousness). It's not surprising, as science putters away in laboratories we have no access to, dropping, on the community far below, articles in journals and newspapers, that the two worlds—one of the lab, the other of the frightened heart—separate further from one another. But Cosmo loved life, treasured his body, was only thirty-five, succeeded in his career, and had much to look forward to. He didn't hate himself, sex, or life. His death did not illumine anything that leaves us morally edified, or superior, or enlightened—it was just part of the vast human waste that is occurring; just mean and nasty.

And though I knew that eventually I would recover from the shock of calling him to return his book, and learning that he was dead, and though I knew this evening I would enjoy my visit to the gym, my optimism—my feeling it was over—was gone. I walked through Union Square up Broadway with a grim expression compressing my lips. All the half-baked theories that ostensibly applied to Cosmo swirled in my mind. None of them worked. I felt more and more despair. And then (as if to supply a literary symmetry to the day), when I got on the track at the Y, I glanced down and saw the gymnastics group working out on the floor beneath—including one handsome Hispanic man doing circles on the pommel horse. Circles are hard to do: You grasp the handles on the pommel, lift yourself up, and swing your legs around above the handles. When it is done well, it looks effortless; the legs themselves seem to be propelling themselves around, faster and faster, as the gymnast moves his hands and travels up and down the horse. It is fluid, graceful, exhilarating. I never learned to do more than one or two, which is to say I never learned circles—though Cosmo did. When I came to New York this spring, I felt we were moving forward—the worst behind us—but now, as the words *Cosmo died* play over and over again in my mind, I think, running ovals around the man doing circles on the pommel horse beneath, in the gym Cosmo loved, *we are getting nowhere at all; we are going in circles.* A pun Cosmo would have liked.

The Names of Flowers

IT'S THE SORT OF PARTY I worked as
a bartender my first few years in the city, and which I
attend as a guest only a decade later. There's someone by
the elevator with a list, checking names when I enter the
building. There's a handsome young man in black tie running the elevator. There's a woman in a bathrobe who says
she got stuck in the elevator between the basement and
the first floor—a neighbor of my host, who goes up with
me to the party in her bathrobe, smelling of Pepsodent. I
never see her again, but the fragrance of toothpaste softens
the formality of the loft filled with guests, the waiters in
black tie, when the elevator operator pulls back the metal
grille and I step forward. The invitation said Food and
Music. Hurrying downtown through deserted streets, later
than I wished to be, I had visions of a concert one could
not enter till the first movement was finished. It is much
more chaotic than that. The thirty-five guests I imagined
are one hundred thirty-five; the music can barely be heard;
the room is roaring. It is a cold April night. There are
sprays of spring flowers throughout the room—more irises
than I have ever seen at one time in a cylindrical glass vase;
strange lilies in a spotlight; flowers whose names I do not
know, which remind me of the Age of Parties—there were
always flowers whose names I didn't know.

Of people I know the names of ten. They are clustered

together in a corner beyond the table on which the glasses are lined up in neat rows beside the bottles and the waiters. I stand there on the edge of the party looking at it like a man selecting a spot on a crowded beach before he puts his blanket and books down, and then I ask one of the two waiters at the long table for a drink. For a long time parties were more enjoyable to me when I worked them than when I came as a guest, but I've not been to a party of this sort in so long, or seen certain friends, that this evening is welcome. "No one has given a party like this in five years!" a friend said on the phone earlier that day. (Parties are like books, like plays: Occasionally the right one comes along at the right time.) This one's got everything: flowers whose names I have to ask, in thin spotlights; a quartet playing chamber music; waiters. It's as if the Age of Parties had been re-created—with one pleasant change: This one doesn't terrify. They used to. I used to attach myself like a leech to the only person I knew in the room—in the Age of Parties I only knew one—till he pried me loose with a lighted match and went off to talk, quite sensibly, to some-one else, at which I felt he had left me alone on a small ice floe, like Little Eva, in full view of the plantation owner's dogs. Now I can stand alone and survey the room before going over to join the group I know—mainly because there is a group I know. No need to panic (though some never did; were poised from the start). It strikes me as I pause there looking at the room, moreover, that this is something to look at a while longer; that what we once took for granted now seems extraordinary.

Even the friends who ten years ago did not know each other now do, and I tell myself to speak with the ones I see once a year, rather than those I saw the previous evening—and this practical thought as I walk over to join them makes me aware, too, of how time has passed. Work-ing a room is not nice. But after many parties one learns there is nothing sillier than the reprimand, once the door has shut behind you, that your life might have been different had you only had the nerve to introduce yourself to Him. Perhaps this time I can introduce myself to the one in the red bow tie: one of several faces I have seen for years but never spoken to, and which now surprise, reassure, and comfort because they are still alive. This is no small achievement in New York in 1985. Life here has assumed the suspense of a summer Sunday's tea dance— you're not sure who is going to disappear on the next boat. In this loft once lived a man who died bravely at home, in complete secrecy, where now more than a hundred people go on with the next installment of the soap opera. He is in some sense still here. He was a handsome, kind, witty man who came to New York from Boston, a famous university, a close-knit family, to write about and live a homosexual life—and he collided with the thing that no artist's dream ever included. It was thought this might be a memorial service, but I learn instead it is a birthday, and the message of the party seems to be: Life goes on, with lots of irises. This seems obvious but is not. I spot an old friend across the room and wonder if I should say hello—because I've not seen him since the mutual friend died. I do and we don't dwell long on the fact. The people who have introduced new mourning customs—replaced wakes with dinner parties at which slides of Fire Island are shown— refuse to give death more than its due. They refuse to be lugubrious. They refuse to be stupid, too, for the most part—and, if before the hidden agenda of these gatherings was the pursuit of sex, now it is the avoidance of it. As a friend said, "No one in New York is having much sex anymore." This makes the party even more curious: An odd reticence pervades the room. What we are not speaking of we are not speaking of by mutual agreement. The collective ego has been dampened. We're all afraid and grateful to be mobile and nervous because we can't say what the future holds. The curious thing is that, though one would think the decision that we are all so vulnerable would make us stay home and give up each other's company—the opposite is true: I enjoy more than ever the sight of homosexuals together. And if a way of life that was once high-spirited, hilarious, is now restrained, solicitous (as if someone went from adolescence to late middle age without the intervening gradations)—we are therefore more grateful for the party. Its taste and generosity and style remind us: Life was once like this. We talk about everything but It. And instead of asking what someone does in bed, we inquire, "Will there be chocolate for dessert?"

For there is more than the names of flowers I do not know as I look out over this noisy, happy crowd. The old assumptions that bound this group together are changed. Our community has been broken up—like the phone company—into different systems of communications. Looking at some of the guests I can tell which ones are celibate; which ones are having little, more cautious sex; and which ones are going right on with the old ways. It has nothing to do with one's degree of personal exposure to the dying; it has to do with temperament, with the way different minds respond to the same facts. We face each other, after all, over freshly dug graves. There are ghosts among us. We're the actresses who meet in the ruined theater in *Follies*. We're tourists who have been admitted to an exhibit of our own former lives. Here are the flowers, the lights, the faces—just as they used to be, when everyone was sleeping with one another. (Gay life without sex is a theme park.) Watching *The Normal Heart* the previous evening, I stared —across the stage between my seat and those opposite— at a handsome man in a long-sleeved, button-down, neatly pressed shirt. He had thick, dark hair; a mustache; watchful, dark eyes; and—beneath his clean clothes—one of those substantial bodies whose broad shoulders, swelling thighs, represent meat, flesh, life. *"Stop screwing!"* the doctor on stage was telling the hero. *"Until this is over!"* And I looked at the man in the first row in the button-down shirt, as if at an éclair on the bakery shelf, and thought, *"Someday, when this is over, perhaps I can have just . . . one . . . more . . . of those."*

That's because there seems to be a lull on this spring evening—which, in this room full of flowers and handsome men, encourages fantasy. Someday life will be as it was again. In fact, on the surface of this city it seems exactly the same. In the past few days I have spent an afternoon in Central Park; seen the Caravaggios at the Metropolitan, the Mayan artifacts at the Museum of Natural History, *The Normal Heart* and *Parsifal* (two works with, strangely, a common theme); had lunch with friends on Second Avenue; watched men meet in my local park at night and leave together; even visited the baths and seen men too numerous to count. Anyone would say nothing has changed. The city goes on: The baths and bars and parks are busy. But there is another city. The doppelgänger that coexists with us: invisible, mental, it draws attention to itself when I pass certain apartment buildings, a baths that has closed, or enter a room in which someone used to live. So if this party seems to re-create a former life—whose felicities we took for granted—there is a mood in the room: the same sentimental delicacy two lovers feel who haven't seen each other in five years but meet in a restaurant they first went to every night the first month of their affair. It's not just that, as another friend said, "New Yorkers have a solution for every dilemma. But not this one." It's that what has happened has left its mark. What has happened to us in New York the past five years has made those who still remain *careful* with each other in a way they weren't before—almost tender. Gone is the old, caustic gossip, the sexual current that lay beneath a party like this to such a degree that reaching for an hors d'oeuvre, you were always wondering, *Who's in the bathroom now, and how long have they been in there?*

That's all passé—and in its place a new reserve based on the simple truth that everyone has adjusted to new facts. Each one of us is Diseased Meat. Diseased Meat is blue-green; it stinks. It makes us think we shouldn't sleep with the man in the red bow tie even if we meet him. Now, there's Clorox and Oxynol-9 and hydrogen peroxide and condoms, and mutual masturbation at ten paces, but that's not what meeting someone in the Age of Parties led to. That's why the Age of Parties ended. That's why it took at least five years for the enormous impetus—the assumptions, standards, freedom, egotism—of Promiscuity, Inc., to slow. The men—who used to be hors d'oeuvres—are no longer edible. So the real hors d'oeuvres become the focus of our mouths. We praise the food, we talk about someone's student days in Paris in the pissoirs that are no longer there, and finally, the cakes on the table lined with bowls of strawberries.

Later someone I've just met remarks he recently began reading a novel by Henry James—a novel in which the heroine dies of an unnamed illness when she is still young, and her life is all before her. The model for this character, it's said, was James's cousin, who died of the disease that in the previous century eclipsed lives before they had run their course or achieved their purpose: tuberculosis. Her death haunted James all his life. The death of people before their time often does. The young writer who lived here had his career still before him; we will never know what he might have written. But it seems to me he was following the advice the doctor gives the heroine of *Wings of the Dove:* "You must be happy. Any way you can!" How ironic! As I look out over the room at the guests, the flowers, the food assembled by a host who brought to his dead lover's illness the same tact and imagination he has shown in re-creating the Age of Parties, I remember something else from *Wings of the Dove*—the very last lines. As the quartet saws away at its instruments in the flower-banked corner, I think of the two lovers who meet each other in the final scene of the book and realize their plan to defraud the heroine of her millions has failed in a way that not only turns their world upside down but introduces a certain estrangement between them. "I'll marry you, mind you," says the man in an attempt to reassure the woman, "in an hour."

"As we were?" she says.

"As we were," he says.

And then, with the finality the plague has introduced to life: "We shall never," she says, "be again as we were!"

That's kind of it. And with this I walk across the room to find my host, whom I half hope not to find, since the right mixture of condolences and gratitude—the referring, or not referring, to the person he's lost; the thank-you for his party—is still not one I've grasped. The room is so crowded I give up with a good conscience. The man in the red bow tie gives me that blank look that seems to convey the sense that men are as nameless and perishable as the flowers I will not learn the names of tonight, either. The tall windows of the loft gaze down on the cold, empty street outside: the street that can no longer promise, when you leave the party, a man to sleep with, in place of the one you did not have the nerve to introduce yourself to here. In the Age of Parties there were lots of substitutes. As I go to the coatroom the refrain of a song that's been going through my mind since this began repeats itself: *The Party's Over*. But is that right? It goes on behind me with laughter and talk and introductions, louder than ever. Perhaps everything *but* the party's over.

Talking to O.

THE FIRST PLACE I saw O. was Central Park—one sunny spring Sunday in the early seventies, after dancing all Saturday night, regrouping with friends the next day in an apartment on Madison Avenue, and then strolling west. The bongo drums were beating in the pool of Negroes around Bethesda Fountain, the nannies from Park Avenue were watching their boys push sailboats across the pond, and clones were converging on the Rambles to cruise, when O.'s retinue was spotted on the horizon of blossoming apple trees. He was a man of medium height, with thick black hair, black eyes, and black mustache—of Hungarian and Turkish parentage. He spoke in a deep, resonant voice, slowly, with a pronounced Turkish-British accent that was, depending on his emphasis, capable of being either very funny or very serious, He had, even on a sunny Sunday in Central Park, surrounded by blossoms, a slightly melancholy, weary air—in those dark eyes, in that rich voice, was a sense of the difficulties of life. When he urged members of his entourage who split off that afternoon to go their separate ways to "Call me tomorrow, at the gallery!" "Don't forget Tuesday night, La Escuelita!" "Irene is coming to town on Wednesday, let's have dinner!" in each conventional exhortation there was an urgency, a seriousness, that might have characterized a father telling his child to watch out crossing the street, and be home in

73

time for dinner. This impression was not far off: O. had brought most of these people from a former life in London and ran a gallery with which several were connected—a gallery that sent O. traveling a lot. But when he was at home in New York, it was at his place that all of them got together.

Food was only part of it. An evening at O.'s involved, above all, conversation—with people one had never met: journalists from Athens, an artist from Mexico City, an old boyfriend of O.'s from Rome. His circle—a circle of friends so constant, so faithful, they had followed one another from city to city and constituted, more than any other I knew, a family—was fixed but fluid, loyal but independent, a function of O.'s affection most of all—his cooking, you might say. Most of them, including O., sold artifacts of one sort or another. But though the world that exchanges art for money is notorious for its meanness, O. was very kind. "Come on up, I am just back from Japan, I want to see you!" he said on the phone. And you went. O. included, invited, charmed, cooked for, and amused so many people that, going uptown to have dinner there, one always felt a bit like a child on Christmas morning—one never knew what would be under the tree.

He was merely the best of hosts—that's all. The Middle Eastern food, the stories about Cavafy, Japan, Lima, the candles, the beautiful room in a brownstone on the Upper West Side we gathered in, were a kind of rosy, glowing tent that O. had set up for his friends. And set up skillfully. Somewhere Santayana distinguishes the arts of poetry, music, painting from the arts of life; the latter are not monuments more lasting than bronze—they last the length of a dinner party—and yet they provide, really, in so many cases, what earthly happiness we have. O. was a master of these. O. embodied that Spanish proverb: "Living well is the best revenge." Once I ran into O. in the hallway of the

Saint Marks Baths, shortly after I had published a book. I was standing in the stairwell of the third floor, brooding about the hopelessness of this cold feast of flesh we gay men had evolved as a way of life, when O. came out of someone's room, beaming. "I have just had a rather wonderful screw," he said, rolling the r. I had not, and dumped on him all the reasons this bathhouse was cold, cruel, alienating, and depressing. O. listened and then said with the faintest smile: "Ah! So success has not made you happy." (Bingo.) His wit, however, did. O. saw things, but saw them without the slightest malice or reproach, so that even your own faults seemed merely human, and less important than the way in which they were phrased. Marriage, said George Bernard Shaw, is a long conversation—so, for that matter, is friendship.

Yet I don't suppose I spoke to O. more than once every three or four months; but when I did—bicycling out to Prospect Park or coming back from Jones Beach on the train—the pleasure was so complete that no matter what we were talking about (the Gulbenkian Museum in Lisbon, the latest sex club south of Fourteenth Street, mutual friends), I think of that decade in part as a conversation with O. And the spell of that spring Sunday in the park —those white apple trees—continued intact, enriched by the passing of time, in each encounter. After leaving Manhattan at the end of the decade, I realized, before very long, how much I missed our conversations, and O. became for me, each return visit, one of the people I could not wait to call. He acquired, in fact, for me, an ideal quality; because I saw him rarely, perhaps, or because he *was* rare, or because he lived in a world different from mine, he became a dream of New York. A dream of New York, dreamt down south, that was harder to square with reality each time I returned. For each time I returned, it seemed everything had changed, changed utterly; even conversations with friends—they, like everything else, sank inevitably beneath the weight of that subject that, though it came last, had banished all humor, liveliness, and joy. The names of the dead, the shock at their number and improbability, the forecasts for the future, the dismal withdrawal and isolation, left one, in the end, speechless. Impotent. There was no way to leave friends in a glow of laughter or affection anymore, there was not even a moral to draw, or an interesting observation, because the plague, with its time lag, its scope, was revealing itself to be some sort of indiscriminate flu, leaving each person alone in a solitary confinement of fear. Conversation, like so much else in New York these past few years, was not much fun.

Perhaps that was why I called O. each time—O. was out of New York as much as he was in it and would be able to describe not only his trip to London, but place in context, perhaps, all that was happening here. "Are you in town?" he said one evening in 1985. "Come by and have supper with us!" Yet the park I walked across that twilight seemed deserted now—a few men sat on the usual benches in the Rambles, seemingly as ignorant as the rats scampering across the path in front of them. And when I got to O.'s, only three of us—O., his boyfriend, and I—sat down in a corner of that large white room, at a small table by the window, in a shrunken pool of lamplight; the rest of the apartment in shadow, like some house whose owners have died, and whose furniture is all under sheets. We ended up discussing, after the amusing topics (the topics that had formed, I realized now in retrospect, the entire menu of our lives), the gloom of the city. "Most of my friends," O. said in a weary voice, "are having trouble negotiating middle age." *What did he mean by this?* I wondered, even as I admired the expression. The city was so full of secrets now—a minefield, and we the mines—I could not be sure what he was referring to. I finally took it on its face: O. meant that the plague was not the only thing happening to New York. Time had passed, too, and even O. had a distinguished silver streak down one side of his thick black hair. AIDS and middle age were but two very different versions of the same thing: dying. The first beyond our power of comprehension, the second all too familiar. So this is what even O. has come to, I remember thinking: middle age. A few months later, I learned this remark was more subtle and detached than that, was only his dry and characteristic way of alluding to something I did not know at the time: While in Japan—fascinated, observant, doing business—he discovered he had AIDS.

When I returned to New York that fall, I called O. from a pay phone on Thirty-fourth Street. It was the middle of an October afternoon; I gathered he was at home alone and asked if I could stop by. I wanted to see O. for several reasons: One, I always wanted to see him; two, I wanted to learn the stage of his illness; and three, I thought I'd better see him one more time—combining, in one uneasy mixture, the past, present, and future. The past: the good times, the happiness. The present: *How far along is he?* The future: *Why didn't you see him, tell him how you feel, let him know you care for him?* (A friend who runs errands, sleeps over, takes someone to the hospital, does not have to say this. Only those who don't wonder how they can.) The park was empty when I walked through it. I had been thinking since I heard the news I should write or phone O. about this fact, but had been unable to find the words. And even now as I walked west, there seemed to be nothing to say that would sound right. I hoped in the act of visiting him that words would make themselves known. I rang the doorbell; the buzzer released the door; I went up the stairs, my heart accelerating not only with the climb; I heard a door open before I reached the top, and a moment later, there was O.—in his socks, looking much the same. We imagine from a distance all sorts of things. I walked in with the familiar pleasure of a child entering a chocolate shop —a place in which everything pleases—surviving even this, and we sat in the big white room and talked.

We talked about the novel he was reading that lay open on the table between us—a historical trilogy about the Balkans by a British writer. Then about mutual friends. And his trip to Tokyo. It was about the Japanese he talked at length in the way I loved: O. was such a good observer. He looked a bit haggard, but not much, and he still talked in the same calm, intelligent, vaguely melancholy, witty way. As he answered my questions about the Japanese, I felt that nothing had changed. Then I changed the topic. And he answered my questions about his health. He discussed the doctors, pneumonia, reactions to medicine (including one that had made his skin peel off), inhalations, alternative therapies. *O.'s life is all doctors now,* I thought as I sat there, *all doctors and hospitals.* He talked about telling his mother. He wanted to visit her, but a doctor had said there was an association between jet travel and the onset of pneumonia in some patients. He had gone to an avant-garde Hungarian whose mixture of medicines had proved a mistake. He was now going to Sloan-Kettering to inhale a medicine that blocked the pneumonia. He stopped finally—after I, completely comfortable, marveling at his enabling me to feel this way, posed yet another question —and asked, "Is this an interview?" He smiled, enjoying the irony, and his eyes sparkled. I smiled, and said, "No."

I wondered as we sat talking if I should, or could, tell O. how much I admired and liked him—but to do this seemed artificial and awkward. So I wondered if he knew without my saying so. And I began to think of Proust's aunts. In *Remembrance of Things Past*, the narrator's two aunts are so horrified by the idea of thanking Swann for the wine he brings them one day—thanking him in an obvious way, that is—that they ignore it altogether, until, shortly before Swann leaves, they slip in a reference to the gift so subtle that only the narrator realizes they are acknowledging the wine, so oblique that Swann leaves oblivious of their gratitude. I sat there thinking O. had given me wine, too—in this very room—a lot of wine, a lot of laughter, a lot of wit, conversation, happiness. But I could no more refer to it now than Proust's aunts could draw attention to Swann's present. Even worse, I didn't want to thank O. for giving me anything; I wanted to thank him for being. (Including· being himself, so wonderfully, now.) And there was certainly no way I could phrase that. So I left. I left O. twenty minutes before his own departure to visit a doctor and refused the tea he offered me, when he went to the stove to turn on the burner, thinking, *There is no need to stay with him. That would be too solicitous.* It was a gray, gloomy afternoon, not one that made being at home alone cheerful; but I was loath to do anything that gave the impression this was a visit in the slightest bit final. I walked down the stairs thinking it had been, after all, but another conversation with O. The huge wooden door closed behind me I left O.'s block refusing to think this might be our last conversation—who could? And what if? There was *still* nothing to say. And I walked east into the park that had been, fifteen years ago, the site of those strolls, those springs, those conversations whose jokes now seemed to have occurred in another language. This Sunday was overcast and gray, the trees still green, and entering this park with that sense of expansion and hope it always gives, I thought, *O. is putting on his coat now to visit the doctor, while I am walking into the park.* The sense of the unfairness of life was then replaced by a sense that I was being followed—by a lean, red-haired man, walking above me on the hill overlooking the Serpentine. I looked back, and we began to circle, like hawks on an air current. We met beneath a copper beech;

we said nothing; I unbuttoned his shirt and ran my hands over his body; he turned away moments later and ejaculated into the air; zipped up, walked off, and disappeared from the park—without saying a word. All the way home the city seemed pervaded by silence.

Cousin Henry

Henry James considered the arch in Washington Square a failure—too modest for its architectural purpose—but walking through the human zoo that congregates around it during the summers in New York, I think of him and it together. White and lordly, remnant of another age, it stands above the mob of break dancers, roller skaters, drug dealers, Frisbee throwers, dog walkers, and jerks who converge there to be hip, with no visible relation to the present. It is one of the few parks I have never even considered cruising—so be-bop is the clientele—but then again, homosexuals rarely linger there Homosexuals circa 1984 are creatures neither it, nor he, ever dreamt of. Yet I dream of him. Passing through the mob on those muggy summer nights, I remember the credo of Lambert Strether in *The Ambassadors:* "Live, live all you can, it's a mistake not to!" And I think, *That is just what I came to New York to do.* When I read the words in college they raised a question—how?—for, like most great instruction, his was left abstract. The novel's solution (Chad Newsome's affair in Paris with a civilized older woman) by my day seemed a bit unnecessary, and anyway the sex was inapplicable. So I came to Manhattan and revised the terms, and found myself, like so many others after the debauch, with the question still unanswered as I walked home from the bars through Washington Square.

One doesn't read a novel by Henry James to learn how to live—not explicitly, anyway. One reads for pleasure. Indeed, in much of his best work, the competing claims of the aesthete and the puritan, the hedonist and the moralist—nowhere more wonderfully wrought than in the stories, and life, of this man—often resolve themselves into a stalemate, a plaintive cry: "I have failed. *You* try!" Max Beerbohm drew a famous cartoon—in which James kneels in a hotel corridor beside two pairs of shoes (a man's, a woman's) trying to peek through a keyhole—that summed up with cruel humor the view of James as a voyeur: a man who wrote novels about remarks overheard at dinner parties. The suspicion has lasted. What engrossed the author of *Washington Square*—reverberations, discoveries, a fire beside which to sort out relationships—the crowd under the arch cannot quite take seriously. Even during his life, and especially toward the end, people wondered, *Did he ever get laid?* The present public expands the question to: *How many times, when, and with whom?* Sophomore year we found a scholar seated alone in the dining hall after delivering a lecture on nineteenth-century American poets; rushed over with our trays, asked if we could sit down; saw him raise his head, still buttering his bread, and say with a weary smile, "*If* you promise not to ask if James was homosexual."

This age asks nothing else and they ask it of the Master especially—a man who loathed the betrayal of privacy so deeply it was, in the James family, the one nearly unforgivable sin. One did not write about one's hosts, one's friends, one's family; one did not betray a confidence—and certainly never in print. This man had so little desire for a biography, he piled his papers on the lawn of Lamb House one day and simply set fire to them all. Henry James was passionately discreet. We are compulsively curious. We look back at him across the abyss of a vanished value system in which privacy was sacred. He stares at us from the portrait by John Singer Sargent with the portly gravity of some banker or prime minister who never saw cockrings, running shoes, and 501s. What can we say to each other, after all? It is true James spent a weekend with Winston Churchill near the end of his life, and visited the wounded of World War I—but he also escorted Ralph Waldo Emerson through the Louvre as a young man, and all his life wrote letters to a woman in Boston who lent her friends copies of Montaigne with the "offensive" pages glued together. Today the Charles is full of condoms. Washington Square is the headquarters of young men rasping "Loose joints, ups, downs," and readers cannot imagine what pages of Montaigne could be offensive. In fact the gap between us is such that to claim he would have written for say, *Christopher Street*, requires a leap of historical imagination so convoluted the mind stalls—it's a little like saying Napoleon would have won at Waterloo had he possessed Exocet missiles, or Queen Victoria, had she been alive today, would have celebrated her Jubilee by dropping acid. Because of this, a certain condescension sets in. And yet he is utterly modern.

Pigeons sit on the arch in Washington Square, after all, as scholars sit on James, too, excreting commentary, and cooing, "*Repressed queen!*" But it's not that simple, despite our confidence in sex as the key that explains everything. Not only the age forbids us—within the age, James constituted a mystery within a mystery. By the end of his life people seemed compelled to deflate James for the same reason Strachey debunked his Eminent Victorians: He was so huge, so unassailable, so proper, so immense, so dignified, so right, so like, in a strange way, Lady Bracknell. His biographer, Leon Edel, whose five volumes I read this summer, wondering how we got from James to Holly Woodlawn so quickly, depicts a young boy (named Angel by his mother) who read books (while his older brother, William, played with the boys, who cursed and swore) and who grew up to be an artist who identified himself paradoxically with the women of his family. They in turn threatened him with their odd mixture of self-effacement and inscrutable force. He decided, not surprisingly, not to marry; saying it would interfere with his career as an artist. His brother, William, put it this way in a letter to his own wife: "Harry is a queer boy, so good and yet so limited, as if he had taken an oath not to let himself out to more than half his humanhood in order to keep the other half from suffering." Such compassion and intelligence—which the Jameses had in abundance—did not characterize most opinions of Henry's Napoleonic celibacy, and the closer he got to the modern age, the more reductive they became.

"An enormous amalgam of the feminine in his make-up," wrote the fashionable New York doctor who treated James for depression after his brother's funeral. "He displayed many of the characteristics of adult infantilism; he had a singular capacity for detachment from reality . . . and a dread of ugliness in all forms. His amatory coefficient was comparatively low; his gonadal sweep was too narrow." Recommended therapy? "Baths, massage, electrocutions." James went, thank God, to another physician; but this was typical. His amatory coefficient and gonadal sweep upset everyone but him. Reflecting on the success James had with London hostesses, a friend wrote, "Henry seemed to look at women rather as women look at them. Women look at women as persons; men look at them as women." James told a story about standing in a street, waiting for a face to appear at a window, while his own was bathed in tears, but it is characteristic of him that he never said if the face was male or female. This reticence frustrated folk who saw—as we do—the key to life in sex. But then James did not. ("The great passion of my life has been the intellectual.") The effect of giving sex the chief role even in a novel, he said in a review, "is that by the operation of a singular law no place seems to be left for anything else; and the effect of that in turn is greatly to modify, first the truth of things, and second . . . what may be left them of their beauty."

Statements like this seem utterly descriptive of life in New York the past ten years, but they led John Addington Symonds a hundred years ago to accuse James of a "laborious beetle-flight" through the garden of sexual identity—no doubt because Symonds was chasing him the way a man runs after a butterfly with a net. He felt James was but couldn't prove it. When William called Henry a "queer" boy, he wasn't using the word the way it is used today. (Yet it is for us a perfect double entendre. James's whole life seems a double entendre.) But he was describing a quality Symonds sensed also. Symonds is one of those figures whose appearance in Edel's biography causes a bell to go off for the homosexual reader. (Oscar Wilde is another. Proust comes at the end, and we never know, unfortunately, what James thought of *Swann's Way*.) Symonds—the author of *A Problem in Modern Ethics* and the Englishman who tried to persuade the Victorian intelligentsia that homosexuality was as valid, as ancient, as the love of man for woman—sniffed around James but got nowhere. (When Symonds wrote to Whitman about *Leaves of Grass*, Whitman was so appalled, he wrote back to say he'd fathered six illegitimate children. Proust for that matter challenged a man who suggested he was an invert to a duel.) There is something comic in everyone's attempt to declare James a homosexual, then and now—especially when Symonds received a book from James with this inscription: "*It seemed to me that sometimes victims of a common passion should exchange a look.*" (The common passion? Italy.)

Oscar Wilde did not even get as far as Symonds; James

found him personally repugnant—"an unclean beast," a fake, a fraud, "a fatuous cad." Santayana on the other hand said he felt an instant understanding during the first ten minutes he spent with James, a rapport he'd not felt all his years with Henry's brother, William. The facts, the hard proof may not be there, but we feel—as Symonds did—that James was, as the French say, sympathetic. And as unperturbed as Inspector Clouseau, leaving one catastrophe after another in his wake: shocked, when Wilde went on trial, not by the charge but the publicity. (That was the real sin.) And yet, while Wilde went down in flames, and James strolled the lawn of Lamb House in the company of two recently arrived American cousins, and he corrects their enunciation, it is he who sounds exactly like Lady Bracknell: "Vow-el, not *vowl*, Rosina."

Rosina (in tears): "Oh, cousin Henry, you are so cruel."

James: "Cru-el, not *crool*, Rosina."

This implacable, orotund voice of propriety—so thrilling in its oracular certitude—is what the young men with whom James is alleged to have slept came to hear. The man they called the Master—of the English novel, and of Lamb House, Rye, Sussex—is the James of caricature and legend; the man who on his deathbed said, "The absence of the male element in my entourage is what perplexes me." Yet the idea that he slept with even one of them borders on the absurd; the only time this might have happened, given James's loneliness when the golden sculptor Andersen appeared, the golden sculptor was so obtuse the possibility never even hovered near reality. The one Gore Vidal nominates—Jocelyn Persse—seems simply to have been a charming young man whose social triumphs reminded James of his own, years before. For the later James, you realize after reading Edel, is but one in a series. He was young once, too; ambitious; in love (with Europe, if not a particular European); full of dreams of glory—many of which came true. To the young men whose youth he basked in, he was kindness itself, applauding their literary and social forays: the wise uncle we all need. (What did the dying James advise his nieces and nephews? Kindness, kindness, kindness.) We may laugh at this role but we miss it too. The words of the American matron to Daisy Miller—"My dear young friend, don't walk off to the Pincio at this unhealthy hour to meet a beautiful Italian" —may sound to us like a line of Ruth Draper's, but in this, the most difficult season of all, when those of us who did go to the Pincio to walk with the beautiful Italian, Puerto Rican, Greek, Frenchman, et cetera, find ourselves more frightened of the Roman Fever than Daisy Miller ever was, we look at the arch, glistening white in its floodlights in the night, and wish he would appear like one of his ghosts to say what we might have made of our society—and point out the mistake.

For it is very odd indeed that the modern reader who snickers over the idea of Daisy Miller dying from the vapors she inhaled watching the moonlight in the Coliseum now learns that life has quite outstripped even Victorian art. One of the most chilling ironies in the biography of Henry James is that, on his last visit to America, he visited a doctor in a hospital where, seventy years later, so many young men who took Strether's advice to live all they could would lie dying: Sloan-Kettering. The doctor took James to his laboratory to show him the behavior of a certain cancerous mouse who had been feeding babies not her own. Just as James was about to speak, someone came through the door and interrupted them; and the doctor realized he would never know what James had been about to say—just as we cannot ask him, "What do you think of the pathology of tricking?" That James himself remained aloof from the passion that obsessed Symonds, ruined Wilde, brought this generation to its crisis, seems clear to anyone who reads his biography. He ended up one of those artists for whom a personal life based on the erotic love of another man was impossible. (Noel Coward and Marcel Proust came to the same conclusion. Love in all three is a topic, an ideal, a disappointment.) When Hugh Walpole—according to Somerset Maugham—offered himself to James, James simply replied, "I can't! I can't!" We will never know why. We can only gawk at the floodlit monument, marooned in the exchange of money and drugs on these humid, amber-tinted nights, and wonder, *Do the bongo drums bother you?* We can simply forage through his life and works, with the occasional shock of recognition, the uncanny sense that he had figured it all out in advance. ("Who are these people," James asked of the characters in a novel a hundred years ago, "who love indeed with fury—though for the most part with astonishing brevity—but who . . . strike us as loving for nothing and in the void?") Or come to a halt when the author in "The Middle Years," who wonders if his work was worth the lifetime he sacrificed to it—as James himself must have, during the dark moments of his later years—finally decides, "It *is* glory, to have been tested, to have had our little quality and cast our little spell. The thing is to have made somebody care."

The professor was right, of course—wanting to know if an artist is homosexual is irrelevant to the work itself—on the one hand. There is more than enough in James's work, life, letters, to turn over and over in the mind and heart. On the other hand, it matters to those faced with con-structing a personal life that asks not whether to live a life based on homosexual relationships but *how.* We read bi-ography, after all, to learn how someone else dealt with the problem of life. How ironic his career seems in this respect! We wonder if there isn't a golden mean between the regrets of a magnificent celibate and our equally for-lorn orgy of sex, each of which leaves one in precisely the same place: alone. In the fiction of James we see the impulse to live blighted by many things—fortune hunters, self-deception, innocence—but the impulse itself is adored and holy. "You've a right to be happy," her doctor tells the worried Milly Theale. "You must make up your mind to do it. You must attempt any form in which happiness must come!" Any form? We stand in the avenue of freedom, like Daisy Miller, Isabel Archer, Ralph Touchett, or Milly Theale, wondering what this could possibly be. It was the question that stumped the student in college, and stumps him still, as impassive, implacable, impervious, immutable as that big white arch.

Tragic Drag

ONE NIGHT IN 1970, I think, friends took me to a very small theater on Tenth or Eleventh Street to see a play called *Hot Ice*. It was a play about cryogenics, and it cost five dollars, I believe; no one explained what we were about to see, yet everyone I went with—people who had seen *Turds in Hell* or *Bluebeard*—had about him a certain air that implied there was no need to explain, I would soon see why one went to any play Charles Ludlam and the Ridiculous Theatrical Company put on.

At the time, I'd stopped going to the theater—mainly because the baths were far more thrilling, more dramatic, and cheaper than anything on Broadway—and because I basically agree with a friend of mine who said theaters should be shut down for ten years and be allowed to open after a decade's darkness if, and only if, there was some justification for it. (And who got up during the second act of a play once and said—when I hissed, "Where are you going?"—"Home, to watch *Masterpiece Theater.*") That was the problem. Sitting in a theater uptown, one was always wondering: *Why did they have everyone drive in from the suburbs, get a baby-sitter, come uptown on the subway, for this? Why couldn't we be at home in our underwear, watching this on TV?* With Charles Ludlam one never asked these questions. Uptown, one found oneself observing people in their living rooms—or, as the "legitimate" theater continued to shrink

from a news-clogged world it could not compete with, their
dining rooms (*Table Manners, The Dining Room*), as if the
family melodrama would someday be distilled down to
single pieces of furniture (*The Bidet*). On the local five
o'clock news you watched, as you dressed for the theater,
a man walking a wire strung between the twin towers of
the World Trade Center; when you got to the theater, you
saw a woman cleaning her house before she committed
suicide. That strange custom of applauding the set when
the curtain went up (so often on a plush Manhattan apartment, reproduced to the last book on the library shelf)
seemed as artificial as the plays on Broadway at the time;
we might as well have been clapping for the designer rooms
at Kips Bay, or the windows at Altman's. At *Hot Ice* there
was no curtain, if I recall; the stage, very small, depicted
the laboratory of a mad scientist (the character that lay
beneath, behind, within, it seemed, almost all the roles
Charles Ludlam took on), and from the moment he came
onstage, I knew something was going to happen.

Nothing is so ephemeral as a theatrical performance—
it even differs from night to night—and, in an age when
songs, concerts, films, books, the explosion of the *Chal-
lenger*, the inauguration of a president, can be reproduced
over and over again, hoarded and stored, what Ludlam
did on his little stage is remembered solely by people
who happened to see him. Writing about him now seems
dumb, like analyzing laughter, which no doubt Ludlam
did, but never in front of us, onstage; in front of us, onstage, he simply induced it. He induced more than that,
however; in any performance of *Camille*, half the people
in the audience were sobbing and half were shrieking with
laughter—at the same line. That was Charles Ludlam. In
a country whose critics, and actors, are always bemoaning
the absence of a repertory company, Charles Ludlam, and
the Ridiculous Theatrical Company he founded, were just

that: a place we could go year after year, to new play after new play, to be entertained. How he did it I don't know. Proust had trouble analyzing Sarah Bernhardt as Berma in *Remembrance of Things Past*—and Ludlam was, like Bernhardt, just an actor. And playwright. And director. And designer. And—it would sound ridiculous, I suppose, if I said genius, but that was how I felt that night in 1970, sitting on the edge of my seat at *Hot Ice*, open-mouthed as any child at a Punch-and-Judy show.

Charles Ludlam *did* a Punch-and-Judy Show, in which he took all twenty-two parts, and that was only one aspect of his theater mania: Nothing in the performing arts was foreign to him, or unused. Puppets, wigs, ballgowns, snoods, musclemen, fake fog, mechanical fish, daggers, goblets, vacuum chambers, flowers, and real flush toilets found places in his theater. His theater was *very*—theatrical. If someone had never seen a play in his life, he could have gone to Charles Ludlam and seen virtually all of theater encapsulated in one performance. Ludlam was comprehensive—pure theater. Which we were starved for—driven to his little group by the staleness of Broadway, the fatuities of a mass-produced, television-dominated, film-and-book-soaked century that gave equal time to the fall of Beirut and the fire in Michael Jackson's hair started by a commercial for Pepsi-Cola. Drowning in what Godard said the West had simply too much of—Culture; on the lam from history, novels, films, the *New York Review of Books*—and none of them any FUN! Grenades ready to explode in our seats when Ludlam came onstage—pins pulled by this short, bald man with a big nose, large dark eyes, and a little mouth. There was something about Ludlam—no matter what the costume, wig, or role, he held you in thrall. There was an insane, cracked quality in this smoldering anarchist of kitsch that made him, no matter what the scene or part, the center of attention. Onstage he had the air of a madman, really, listening to some lurid music of the spheres the rest of the cast could not hear. This performer, who looked, on the street, like the superintendent of an apartment building on Jane Street, or a janitor sweeping up at a high school on the Lower East Side, or a salesman who sold trusses out of an office in midtown Manhattan, was, when he came onstage, an actor so charismatic, so in possession of his method, that no matter how bad the play—and there were a few one did not *rush* to recommend to friends—or how mundane the particular passage, one never took one's eyes off him. Ludlam—and his *gothic* eyes—always seemed at the least perturbed; at most, as loony as Rasputin.

The greatest comedy has this element of madness, perhaps—the sense that we've shoved off, there are no limits, the actor is wacko. (Mel Brooks, not Woody Allen; Richard Pryor, *not* Bill Cosby. *Never* Bill Cosby.) Lunacy and cunning pulled Ludlam's chariot with competing force. The saying "Life is a tragedy to those who feel, a comedy to those who think," is too schematic, after all. Because most of us think *and* feel, if not always simultaneously, the pressure of the two creates an urge in some of us to just—*lose it* now and then. That's what the cult of Dionysus was all about, and the cult of Dionysus is where Theater started. You could lose it with Charles Ludlam. It would be pointless to subject Ludlam to a dissertation—he was too funny—and yet no one was more grounded in theater's ancient roots than he; like a child running through the contents of his bedroom closet, putting on fake noses, mustaches, pulling out toy airplanes, little plastic gladiators, goldfish bowls, ray-guns, Cleopatra wigs, he always gave the impression of having assembled the particular play from a magic storeroom in which he kept, like some obsessed bag lady, every prop and character that two thousand years of Western history had washed up on the shores of a childhood on Long Island. If uptown you watched depressed people in their living rooms, when you went to the little theater that became Ludlam's permanent home, you sat down before a palace in Carthage, a temple, a crypt, a tomb, a railroad station, a yacht cruising the Aegean with billionaire and diva taking the sun—everything *but* the living room: Instead of a *hausfrau* committing suicide, Camille in Paris, gayer times, other centuries, cultures, codes of conduct: the gamut of Western culture's books, plots, and characters. Ludlam added subjects, when the theater was subtracting them, introduced new plays, when the houses uptown were dark for lack of original work, became more theatrical when most of the lore and craft of theater seemed to have slipped away to Hollywood.

Ludlam did make movies—even appeared in a television sitcom I tuned to once by accident—but his genius belonged to the theater. Theater was his *subject*. He mined past plays, for his exaggerations, intonations, looks, monologues, asides, settings, props. He made fun of all its pretense. Once Ludlam sat down on a toilet onstage in *Stage Blood,* delivered Hamlet's soliloquy, stood up, pulled the chain, and in that single flush sent up every apartment erected on a Broadway stage. In Ludlam, realism was make-believe; make-believe was the joke (and the delight)—so that we gasped when, as a Carthaginian princess about to be purified before her marriage in *Salammbo,* he raised his skirt to reveal what looked like a vagina for ritual shaving. And we thrilled when the cardboard train came sliding onstage to deliver Galas (the diva whose first line, at the station café, was, "I'll have the veal cutlet"). The make-believe train was the sort of thing children would be delighted by, but then that is what we all were, at a Ludlam play: children. Smart, jaded, ironic, sophisticated children, watching a magician dress up, caress, and bring to life again a theater whose corpse the "legitimate" theater was too sophisticated, too tasteful, too realistic, too something to rouse.

It seems that simple: Ludlam *used* theater—its most ancient, vulgar tricks—when no one else was able to. He did so, chiefly, by making fun of it. That was all he needed to give us entrance to realms one could no longer visit any other way. The god of originality in the arts, after all, is mean: One can no longer offer up on his altar a sonata like Schubert's, a play in iambic pentameter, a poem like Keat's. One can only write *The Importance of Being Earnest* once. (So today we get electronic music, and Julian Schnabel.) Ludlam found a way around the altar—had a key that unlocked the door of that chamber behind the deity in which all those heroes and heroines, villains and viragos (Camille, Bluebeard, Hamlet, Wagner, Callas—and Houdini) were waiting to amuse us again. The key, the rejuvenating alchemy, was Satire. Farce. A unique aesthetic in which the classic became avant-garde. Who else but Ludlam would have staged an obscure novel by Flaubert as a send-up of Hollywood epics about gladiators with the sort of chests that made Groucho Marx say he never went to films in which the men's tits were bigger than the women's? (Ludlam merely hired a group of muscle builders from a local gym.) Who else but Ludlam would have given us *Camille?* With such conviction—such art—that half the audience was laughing while the other half groaned, and what the audience was doing changed from moment to moment, line to line, syllable to syllable, as we followed the rises and dips of that incredible voice—that resonant, dark, wounded, demonic, sinuous, whimsical, whining, wheedling, imperious instrument?

Ludlam was above all a master of the punch line—the mainstay of Woody Allen—which punctured the balloon of High Art but fast. (When Camille is dying, her lover Armand ends a florid declaration of his love with the words,

"Toodle-oo, Marguerite!" When Galas lists the reasons she wants to die, the last one is, "And there's nothing on television tonight!") But the punch lines came only after we'd drunk rapturously of the Real Thing. One may ask, "What did we know of the Real Thing?" "Tragedy is dead," said the critic. We could no longer stage this seriously. Our teeth were fluoridated, our theater air-conditioned. Too modern, too rational, too prosperous, too aware of genocide to care about individual fate. Why, then, did we sit rapt before dying Camille? Ludlam, all those years when the theater uptown was either Las Vegas vulgar or dead, was our only showcase of the bravura roles, the classic acting of a sort one could no longer find, in the Age of Realism—in a culture whose solution for grief is grief counseling, whose reaction to catastrophe is stress management and acupuncture, Ludlam played Tragedy. He played both Tragedy and Farce and refused to tell us which was which. He died onstage of tuberculosis, or heartache, and left us not knowing whether to laugh or cry, suspended somewhere (with parted lips) between the two; so that when he raised his gloved hand to his lips, as Camille, and coughed those three little coughs—just three—the audience both howled and stopped laughing altogether.

He also performed at a time when what was underground and what was homosexual were one—there was a whole decade, after all, between Candy Darling and Harvey Fierstein—and his two greatest roles were basically Tragic Drag: women whom fortune dumps in a rather rude way—Camille (whom Ludlam played more than once, a favorite he could always resurrect) and Galas. It seems now in retrospect that all art presupposes a certain health, leisure, freedom in which to laugh at things that in Life are actually horrid and brutal. We all could scream at the three little coughs which caused earlier generations to sob—or Galas's lament, "Everyone I know is either dead or in Monte

Carlo!"—because at the time we were worried primarily about our *latissimus dorsi*. Ludlam was described to me, in fact, that night I saw *Hot Ice*, as an ornament of gay New York—like the Loft, the Everard—pleasures of a segment of society that in 1970 was Fun. In the theater that night were people who had come to the city, to work and play, for whom Ludlam was the adored genius whose next play (no tortured intellectual he, observing long periods of silence before he had something new to say; Ludlam put on plays the way bakers bake bread) was a piece of news joyously transmitted in the hallways of the baths. When Ludlam turned, in *Camille*, to his maid in a boudoir in Paris and said (in that ruminating, pathetic tone), "Throw another faggot on the fire!" whole ages of repression went up in shrieks. ("There are no faggots in the house, Madame," the maid replied respectfully. And Ludlam, rising on one arm on the chaise longue to look directly out at his audience with that morose expression would say, "What? No *faggots* in the house?")

There were lots of faggots in the house, of course—bronzed, muscular habitués of gyms and Fire Island, in plaid shirts, muscles, and mustaches—and if everything Ludlam did was ironic, a double entendre of sorts, so were their lives, and Camille and Galas spoke to that. Ludlam was superb in a lot of other roles (*Le Bourgeois Avant-Garde, Salammbo, The Mystery of Irma Vep*), but there were plays I let run without making the effort to see, because they were merely satire, or, as a friend fumed one time when I asked how the new one was, "hardly high school." (Some high school! What Bluebeard said might apply as a small understatement to Ludlam's work: "When I'm good I'm very good, and when I'm bad, I'm . . . not bad.") *Camille* and *Galas*, however, were of another order. Drag is a profound joke—the fundamental homosexual joke, no doubt: the Woman at Bay, Wounded but Triumphant, lascivious or frigid, repressed or mad, rings all the notes, high and low. That which appalls the race in real life (change of sex roles) onstage unchains. Charles Ludlam was the greatest drag I've ever seen. It ceased to be drag, in fact, or acting: it was art. That mouth, those eyes—that voice, that fan! That insidious send-up of absolutely everything! That superb evocation of the classic, the romantic, the aristocratic. (Yes, aristocratic. The secret wish of every homosexual—the drag queen as Queen. Of the *Universe*.) We sat in our jeans and T-shirts in a city, culture, and century flooded with fake emotion and took *Camille* utterly seriously—the only way we *could* take it: as a joke.

Alas, the veneer of culture is quite thin, and make-believe no match for reality. The misery of nineteenth-century tuberculars is no longer a subject for exquisite farce; and this generation—for whom tragedy could be performed only *as* farce—is now having to separate them again, and put farce in the attic. Not only is Charles Ludlam gone, it seems, so is humor. One no longer can make jokes about death. One can no longer make jokes at all—the curtain's down. Talleyrand is supposed to have said that those who never lived before the Revolution never knew *douceur de vie*—well, those who never saw Charles Ludlam before the plague missed some brilliant moments in the theater. Oh, were they brilliant. Oh, was he funny. Oh, is he dead. Oh, is this plague—ridiculous.

(Artificial) Marble

GEORGE SANTAYANA'S ONLY novel, *The Last Puritan*, was a best-seller when it was published in 1936: Number one for several weeks, nominated for the Pulitzer Prize (a book no one remembers won), it interested Paramount Pictures (it somehow seems unfilmable), sold 148,000 copies in hardcover, and prompted one critic to remark that it was the finest book that had yet come out of America. Now it is out of print. I read it years ago only because a college instructor suggested I do so; since *The Last Puritan* is a novel of education—in particular, the education of a young American named Oliver Alden. Santayana worked on it desultorily over the course of forty-five years, and its slow, leisurely depiction of the shaping of a soul reflects a lifetime of meditation on questions for which students in every age feel an urgent need to find answers. It also appeals to anyone who loves lucent, graceful prose. Santayana was that exception among philosophers, after all: a man who made his living from his books; one of the great stylists. During his lifetime he was both famous and read, and if now he is less so, that is our loss, John McCormick says in his new biography of Santayana. He closed his book with the comment of an admirer: "What happens to Santayana's reputation will be a touchstone of the quality of our culture, and of our growth in maturity and wisdom." In his introduction, McCormick adds that if this biography gets us simply to read Santayana's works, it will have succeeded. For he means to refute the critics who during his lifetime dismissed Santayana for being something less than a philosopher ("Why should we let this dainty and unassimilated man tell us how to live?"), to bring Santayana back to the center of the stage he occupied when he was alive—and he was alive a very long time, dying in 1952 at eighty-eight.

His life spanned an extraordinary period of historical change, in fact: He was born in 1863 (in Madrid) at the time of the American Civil War, and he died (in Rome) just after the Korean conflict. I use these events because we think of him as an American figure, and yet all his life he carried a Spanish passport and described his own past as uprooted. His parents were Spanish. But his mother's first husband—whom she met while living in the Philippines—was a Bostonian named Sturgis, and she promised to raise their children in Boston should anything happen to him. It did: He died. So this proud, dour woman, to whom none of her children, Santayana wrote his beloved elder sister, ever "came up to snuff," kept that promise, even after marrying a second time; and, after settling in Spain with her second husband (Santayana's father), she removed the children of her first marriage to live in Boston, leaving Santayana behind with his father to live in Avila. Then, at the age of eight, he too was sent to Boston to live among the Sturgises, where he excelled in the Boston Latin School and Harvard College. On graduation he took a teaching position at the latter. Years later he explained his decision to pursue—*faute de mieux*—an academic career: "I was fond of reading and observation, and I liked young men." (This might describe his whole life.) When his mother's death freed him from Boston, however, he resigned his post teaching philosophy at Harvard and went to Europe, free of academic duties and protestant Boston, and wrote books. Many books. His major professional work ran to five volumes and was called *The Life of Reason*. He also wrote poems (when young), plays, a novel, essays, a memoir in three volumes, dialogues, soliloquies, a book on politics. He wrote through two World Wars—the first spent in England, the second in Rome—and finally settled in a convent in the latter city run by the lyrically named Blue Nuns, and died there in 1952.

"While his life was not a dramatic one," reads the copy on the dust jacket of this biography, "—it was too austere and disciplined—it was rich in its interior dimensions and outer associations." In other words: His life was the life of the mind. And yet, for a philosopher—a retired professor—Santayana moved in worldly company. Santayana both studied under and taught with William James. Henry James said he would have walked miles through the snow to meet him, when he finally did. A. E. Housman, Bertrand Russell, Bernard Berenson, Robert Lowell, Ezra Pound, Rockefeller—with whom Santayana watched the Jubilee of Queen Victoria—also appear. Santayana moved with ease much of his adult life in the world of big hats and bigger lawns. Yet never envying the rich their possessions—he seemed to have needed only a hotel room in which to write—maintaining his habits (of reading, writing, traveling) while everything else around him changed. His life—too "austere and disciplined" to be "dramatic"—was that of the observer.

And the observation was shrewd, wise, and very gracefully expressed: Santayana's writing is so conversational, subtle, and charming that even in *The Last Puritan* nearly every third or fourth sentence is an aphorism one wishes to commit to memory. Yet Santayana is more than a necklace of *pensées*. When an admirer of his published a book during his lifetime containing fragments from Santayana's writing, Santayana told a friend he was "disgusted with it."

The man's selections, Santayana said, were not diversified: "too much commonplace rationalism (when I am not a rationalist) and not enough cynicism or skepticism or psychological malice . . . witless criticism of religion, without all the pages of sympathetic treatment of it . . . I was furious." In short, it is not easy to summarize, classify, extract, or even explain Santayana, a man who, every time someone tried to claim he was a cynic, a pessimist, a Catholic, an ascetic, a Stoic, an Epicurian, a Fascist, a Spaniard, an American, a Platonist, a materialist, a pragmatist, took pains to show how he differed from each. Santayana once compared philosophers to men shopping for a pair of shoes that fit. He himself seems to have found none he liked. In the opinion of admirers like McCormick, however, Santayana had—despite the suspicion of other philosophers—a system of his own that was original. (In his essays "A Brief History of My Opinions" and "On His Friendly Critics," Santayana explains it about as succinctly as one could wish. No one described his own oeuvre better than he did, in fact, when he said he spent his life saying "unEnglish thoughts in English.") Much of Santayana's work on philosophical subjects is fairly technical, however. And to the modern lay reader, Santayana's definitions of Reason, Essence, Truth, Spirit, Will, and so forth, seem almost as academic as the very thinkers Santayana disdained for their self-absorption and narrowness. But this is no obstacle. For if Santayana's definition of Essences does not compel the reader, his views of poets, playwrights, novelists—of history, civilizations, human nature—do; if one does not read Santayana's philosophical works, one can find that philosophy beautifully expressed in his perceptions as a critic.

Santayana was a critic par excellence all his life—a sort of *arbiter elegantiarum* of thought. And his criticism flowed from his philosophy, which was that of a naturalist who wished to know himself and the world he lived in. ("The good is the perfection of life for each creature according to its kind; a perfection which man can never reach without knowledge of his immediate circumstances and his own nature.") A naturalist, to put it quickly, says, "What is, is." (Including the atom bomb: Hiroshima and Nagasaki were "disasters, no doubt," he wrote a friend. "But so is the eruption of Mount Vesuvius a disaster.") Of course, the mind that considered atom bombs and volcanoes equivalent was criticized as pessimistic, disillusioned, and detached.

There was an unspoken feeling that Santayana was *too* reasonable, perhaps—"abnormal," in the opinion of the president of Harvard considering his promotion—divorced from mere human needs and appetites. McCormick wishes to correct this impression, to show us a man who (though careful all his life to maintain his independence—of universities, relatives, philosophic feuds, and, it seems, sex) considered himself the same material he saw all around him in other minds and hearts, subject no more and no less to the same discerning and, in the end, accepting eye. One day, for instance, Santayana remarked calmly to Daniel Cory, his personal secretary, concerning the poetry of A. E. Housman, "I suppose Housman was really what people nowadays call 'homosexual.' I think I must have been that way in my Harvard days—although I was unconscious of it at the time." Though McCormick suggests the last statement is disingenuous—he says Santayana was too worldly not to have known—a letter written to a friend in 1887 when he was still at Harvard gives us a glimpse of a man who was both self-conscious and intensely romantic: "What I crave is not [to] do great things, but to see great things. And I hate my own arrogance and would worship the man who should knock it out of me. Says a Spanish song:

> I was searching land and ocean
> For the man that I might love
> And whenever my heart finds
> him
> Then he will have found his slave

Man or thing—it makes no difference—but heaven grant it be no woman."

Santayana was granted his wish, in one sense, at least: It was no woman. It was probably not a man either, despite the part played in his life by Frank Russell, an English aristocrat Santayana met when he was still an instructor at Harvard. Russell was booted out of Oxford on suspicion of having had sex with a man in his room—a fact Santayana transferred to Lord Jim, and the Navy, in *The Last Puritan*—though Russell went on to live an intensely messy heterosexual life whose oafishness finally disillusioned Santayana. He seems to have captivated Santayana for a while, however. In the youthful spring of 1887, Santayana wrote, "While at Oxford, I hope to meet some more specimens of the English race, thanks to Lord Russell, who has been a godsend to me. I don't tell you anything about my adventures with him because I have to maintain with you my reputation as a philosopher, and in this respect I have quite lost my reason. When I am safely in Spain again, and can treat the matter objectively, I will make a full confession of my fall—from grace and self-control I mean and not into the Thames, although this also is mortifying enough. . . ."

Fall from grace, self-control—that such a loss of reason would be "mortifying" gives us a clue, perhaps, to how Santayana viewed sexual obsession: disapprovingly. "Dante was one of the masters," he wrote in *Three Philosophical Poets*, "because he discovered the necessity of saying continually to oneself: Thou shalt renounce. And for this reason," Dante "needed no other furniture for hell than the literal ideals and fulfillment of our absolute little passions." Our absolute little passions—though they seem to constitute the whole of life for many moderns—Santayana did not set much store by. Of all the motives in philosophy and life, romantic egoism earned his sharpest scorn. Not because Santayana never felt its force himself: An American sergeant who visited the philosopher in Rome recalled Santayana in 1946 telling him "the 'Tiger of the flesh' (sensuality/sexuality) never dies. Presumably, then, it had not died in him."

All his life Santayana appreciated the presence of handsome young men; when he was an aged celebrity in Rome, when he was a young instructor at Harvard. (It was Santayana's view that people do not change over the course of a life very much: "Only mediocrities," he said, "develop.") All his life he used the word *manly* as one of approbation: As a young graduate student in Berlin, he disliked Germany, but not the men marching down the street in uniform. One element of Santayana's famous detachment, if that is what it was, may have been that of the lover of men who refuses to make love to them because that would be unmanly. Such hearts can love under the guise of friendship. Friendship was important to Santayana. *The Last Puritan* is shot through with the poignance of an attachment between two young men that cannot be translated into erotic terms. Santayana was fond of several of his students, to whom Santayana's letters, written on the occasion of their engagement to women, are both touching and comic. When visitors beat a path to his door in Rome—when everyone from American sergeants to Gore Vidal came to call on him (the latter brought Tennessee Williams and Samuel Barber)—Santayana seemed to have responded to them along the same lines: whether they were (a) male, (b) good-looking. ("I have had the unexpected

pleasure of seeing Bob," he wrote, of a great-nephew,
"—a big, strapping handsome fellow.") One American sergeant who stopped by could not decide whether Santayana
was smiling at him because he was turned on or simply in
a good mood: "Santayana reputedly was homosexual. Perhaps he was, or perhaps this is only a libel on his memory.
He seemed to smile at me a lot; but possibly this was only
the outward mark of a sunny disposition." (Why not sex
and a sunny disposition? And no, it is not libel to suggest
he found you pleasant to look at.) Homosexuality seems
never to have presented a moral problem to Santayana, at
any rate, any more than any other natural fact—and Santayana never made of himself a fool for Beauty.

Instead, the man who wrote "Life is an exercise in self-
government" admired the Greeks, equated harmony with
reason, pointed out that the ancients' ideal in life was not
freedom but wisdom, and seems for these reasons to be
light-years away from modern life. (Consumers are parasites, Santayana said; industrialism condemns men to the
bar and brothel; liberalism is egoism.) At some point in his
life, in the same way that he decided he would give up
writing sonnets, Santayana must have decided to surrender
his search for that man who could enslave him. One is
tempted to use Nietzsche's categories—Apollonian and
Dionysian—to describe the problem. Compare Santayana
with Joe Orton, for instance, a figure who seems so much
closer to us, wandering the latrines of London, going to
Morocco for the boys. Orton celebrated, explicitly, in his
work and life, Dionysus. Santayana valued self-control and,
even in war, when the gas chambers, bombs, burning cities
were all scenes of the most destructive absolute little passions imaginable, remained in his room in Rome con-
densing *The Life of Reason;* Apollo as Castillian monk,
Epicurus as trapped expatriate; not the Epicurus of popular myth (the man who knows the best caviar), but the

Epicurus who believed the object of morality (Pleasure) was derived from a life of prudence, honor, and justice. Behind the lines, miles from the atrocities, Santayana continued to suggest that harmony and self-restraint were essential to human happiness.

But the point *was* to be happy: "There is no cure for birth or death but to enjoy the interval," he wrote. Santayana had nothing to do with self-flagellation. "Survival is something impossible but it is possible to have lived and died well." Perhaps the problem is we have made living well synonymous with what feels good; our economy depends on it. Dying well is something we have somehow forgotten, too. (Santayana's essay "War Shrines" in his book *Soliloquies in England* speaks perfectly to the present, when youth is dying as senselessly as in World War I.)

And yet this reasonable approach to the problems of birth, death, suffering, made—and still makes—people impatient, even annoyed. Santayana refused to join philosophers in their internecine debates—or even the usual emotional reactions to things. When word of Russell's death reached him in 1931, Santayana "reacted to the news not at all." And Cory asked, "Mr. Santayana, if I dropped dead in front of you, would you be emotionally moved at all?" Santayana replied, "You should not ask me personal questions." (We could end our expedition right here, with this remark; but there is nothing rational about the curious desire to know more about the author of works of art that move us.) "Then he appeared to relent a little," Cory goes on. " 'I knew Russell a long time ago. And the man I knew and loved then died, I am sure, many, many years ago.' " This was in keeping with Santayana's view that all life—civilization as well as people—was taken on the wing; an acceptance of life's ephemerality reflected in one of his titles, *My Host, The World*, which sounds as if he were only a guest at some house party. Where exactly did he reside?

When people were discomfitted by Santayana, they said (in America) he was Spanish, and (in Spain) he was American—but it was precisely this outsider status that defined him.

Did he—like Shylock—bleed? Had he—feelings? No doubt. (Writing to William James about James's review of a book, Santayana complained that James had missed the *tears* that lay behind his words—this from a man who never used one carelessly—and elsewhere said that what he most saw was the *pity* of love.) "To be detached from the world without hostility," Santayana wrote in an essay. And yet: "What I suffered from," in a letter late in life, "was distaste for the world." Santayana seems to have thought early on that life was "hideous." Like that other famous citizen of Avila, it is quite possible that—though he denied it—he was temperamentally at least a mystic, a mystic who could not believe in God, the person in that Spanish song searching land and sea for someone to serve. Not only did Santayana shrewdly maintain his independence throughout his adult life—from relatives, politics, universities, and sex—he was careful to the end to guard himself against encroachment by the Church his freethinking father so disliked; before his death, leaving explicit instructions that, even if Extreme Unction were brought and he seemed to nod, it must not be construed as a conversion; refusing to donate the flowers in his sickroom to the convent altar for fear it would cause a rumor he had converted; replying, when asked if he wanted an audience with the pope: "I never seek out celebrities." (Santayana, meet Sister Boom-Boom.) Imagine for a moment the religious spirit—so like the romantic one—denying itself its passionate impulse (to worship, adore) because it could not rationally believe in God. Imagine, too, the homosexual self—so like the religious one—denying itself its passionate impulse (to worship, adore) because it was unmanly, "mortifying" to lose self-control. ("Life is an exercise in self-government.") Those to whom the loss of self-control has been a goal might wonder if these two coincided here. How else to explain him, except that he was wiser than the rest of us? But one can only amuse oneself with these ideas. If Truman Capote, when asked what he thought of John Updike's writing, compared it to "smoke," then Santayana's persona and prose might be likened to the sky in which smoke loses itself, filled with monumental clouds, shifting with air currents and moisture and sunlight throughout the day.

Santayana was large, and skillful, and private, and McCormick's biography—as thorough and complete as it is—only sends you back to Santayana on your own. While reading it I searched nevertheless for the one offhand, telling remark, or action, or scene, from some unofficial, casual source that would clarify his elusive character. The closest occurred perhaps during the visit of another American soldier following the liberation of Rome who—this time—took Santayana for a ride around town in his Jeep. ("Love has never made me long unhappy," Santayana wrote to a friend in 1929, "nor sexual impulse uncomfortable; on the contrary, in the comparatively manageable form in which they have visited me, they have been great *fun*, because they have given me an interest in people . . . things, places, and stories . . . which otherwise would have failed me altogether; because in itself, apart from the golden light of diffused erotic feeling falling upon it, the world I have been condemned to live in most of my life would have been simply deadly. I have never been anything but utterly bored and disgusted with the public world, the world of business, politics, family, and society. It was only the glimmer of sport, humour, friendship, or love falling over it that made it tolerable.") That afternoon in Rome, Santayana sat eating, in the golden light, a flavored ice "like a schoolboy," in the Jeep, telling the captain, among other things, that of all the statues in the Pincio, only two were of women. As he drove around the liberated city—with this soldier who, unlike the Roman who slew Archimedes, had come to converse—Santayana "would point to piles of stones with the explanation 'Those are fake.' 'Those are real.' " There—sitting in a Jeep with Captain Martinez, eating ice, appraising ruins: a man who, even after collapsing on the steps of the Spanish consulate (the last time he left the convent of the Blue Nuns, to renew his passport), noted in a letter to a friend that the steps he broke three ribs on were "(artificial) marble." All his life Santayana pointed out what was real and what was fake—in marble, religion, art, philosophy, politics, morality. Shortly before his death, when Cory asked him if he were suffering, Santayana answered, "Yes, my friend. But my anguish is entirely physical; there are no moral difficulties whatsoever."

Notes on Promiscuity

1. IF A YOUNG man is promiscuous, we say he is *sowing his oats;* if a young woman is promiscuous, we say she is a *slut*; if a homosexual of any age is promiscuous, we say he is a *neurotic example of low self-esteem.*

2. Everyone has his/her own definition of promiscuity.

3. A person who is promiscuous professionally is a prostitute. Most people who are promiscuous would be shocked if you called them a prostitute, however, because they do not think of themselves that way, simply because they do not charge money.

4. There is a tribe of people in Uganda so promiscuous that the name of the tribe is also the word for prostitute.

5. Promiscuity is thought of in two ways: as having many, many different partners; and as having no standards for the people with whom one sleeps. The second type is comparatively rare, however, and is held in contempt by the first. The worst thing we can say about someone is that he/she will sleep with *anybody.*

6. But the truth is that many of us will sleep with *almost* anybody.

7. In ancient Rome, a certain empress would slip out of the palace at night, Juvenal tells us, to take a room in a local brothel and entertain customers till dawn. This was being both promiscuous *and* a prostitute. (*And* bored.) (*And* an empress.)

8. Sex is a pleasurable experience repeated many, many times during our lives that, if experienced with the same person each time, is considered responsible, adult, mature; if experienced with a different person each time, is considered promiscuous.

9. Americans, products of a consumer society, with a short attention span, a bent for instant gratification inculcated by advertising, and a fairly lonesome society, are *made* for promiscuity.

10. Some gay men think promiscuity is a revolutionary ideal that can transform the world, release human energy, and make the planet a better place to live.

11. Others think promiscuity is the freeway to hell.

12. It takes time to become promiscuous. Married couples reading stories about AIDS are astounded to learn that a homosexual man has slept with eight hundred men; to the homosexual reader, this does not seem *that* bizarre.

13. The word for promiscuity in gay life is *tricking*.

14. Tricking depends on motive—one may not consider oneself promiscuous at all, for instance, though at the end of ten years of tricking you've slept with many people.

15. (Once, when someone asked me, "Do you consider yourself promiscuous?" I realized that though I'd slept with a number of different people, I had never considered myself promiscuous.)

16. Before the plague, promiscuity was a growth industry.

17. Before the plague, promiscuity was the sore point of homosexual life. Why—even gay men wish to know— did homosexuals convert liberation into promiscuity?

18. No one knows.

19. When a friend asked me, "Why are gay men promiscuous?" I started to reply, "Because they don't marry and have children, because they feel guilty about being gay, because they're men, because men are like dogs, because they're lonely, because everyone would have as much

sex as he could if he could, because sex is the most tran-
scendent experience"—then I saw my friend lighting another cigarette, and said, "Why do you smoke?"

20. Promiscuity was the *lingua franca*, the Esperanto, of
the male homosexual community.

21. Men are now weeping in doctors' offices over the
fact that they were once promiscuous.

22. Men are now telling other men in the new cities
they've moved to that they never *were* promiscuous.

23. (Gay men now *suspect* each other of promiscuity.)

24. Gay men have been blamed for the plague by people
who say promiscuity caused AIDS.

25. But promiscuity flourished in the seventies precisely
because it *was* disease-free (or so everyone thought). That
is, every disease acquired via promiscuous sex was curable
with some form of penicillin.

26. In fact, promiscuity's considerable charm may be
measured by the number of afflictions people were willing
to put up with as the *occupational hazards* of promiscuity.
Until AIDS, these were: crabs, scabies, venereal warts,
syphilis, gonorrhea, anal fissures, amoebiasis, hepatitis, and
(the first one to give promiscuous heterosexuals pause)
herpes.

27. Once, while leaving the public health clinic on Ninth
Avenue, I asked a friend how he was going to celebrate
the test results that showed he had finally rid himself of
intestinal parasites, and he replied, "By going to the Mineshaft tonight." Such was the allure of promiscuity.

28. Promiscuity is now inseparable from the dread of
AIDS.

29. Yet promiscuity must be separated from the issue of
AIDS if one wants to evaluate it, because no one in the past
was promiscuous knowing it would lead to what it led to.

30. People were promiscuous in the past for a simple
reason: "Sexual practices are banal, impoverished, doomed

to repetition," Roland Barthes said, "and this impoverish-
ment is disproportionate to the wonder of the pleasure
they afford."

31. And: "I have spoken of pleasure," wrote Renaud
Camus in his introduction to *Tricks*, "but I don't see what . . .
would keep me from calling such moments happiness."

32. And: "How can we not desire, afterward, to encounter similar moments once again, even if only once
more?"

33. *Once more* (or *Once Is Not Enough*) is the *mantra* of
promiscuity.

34. The motto of promiscuity is: *So Many Men, So Little
Time.*

35. The slogan of promiscuity is: *Show us your meat.*

36. Many celebrated people, including presidents, have
been promiscuous—John F. Kennedy, for example.

37. Very few homosexual men are not or have never
been promiscuous.

38. The nature of promiscuity came clear to me the night
at the baths when I looked back at the doorway of the
room whose occupant I had just fallen deeply in love with
after the most wonderful, intense, earth-shattering, intimate, and ecstatic sex and watched another man walk into
his room and close the door behind him with a little click.

39. Promiscuity offends that deep desire W. H. Auden
said was not merely to be loved, but "to be loved alone."

40. Promiscuity entails a double standard: We want to
be promiscuous ourselves, but we want the people we sleep
with to want only us.

41. The average person thinks other people have sex
with him because he is good-looking, sexy, special, attractive. In a promiscuous world, however, we are picked up
mostly because we are *breathing*.

42. The first law of promiscuous physics is: Over a long
enough period of time, everyone sleeps with everyone else.

43. The second law of promiscuous physics is: Every face is new to someone.

44. The third law of promiscuous physics is: The thousandth trick is not what the first one was.

45. There is no telling where promiscuity would have led homosexual men had the plague not occurred; it is possible it might have faded away, as people grew tired or disillusioned with it; or it is possible people would have started coming to work—as a friend predicted—"with broken arms."

46. When asked why he was moving from New York City to San Francisco in 1978, a friend of mine said with an ironic smile, "To improve the quality of my promiscuity."

47. He is now dead.

48. Tennessee Williams said, "Each time I pick someone up on the street, I leave a piece of my heart in the gutter."

49. Oscar Wilde said, "I lie in the gutter, but look up at the stars."

50. (Now that it is denied them, people realize how romantic promiscuity was.)

51. Promiscuity gave rise to two terms of gay slang: *fast-food sex* and the *sex junky.*

52. No one can ever be sure why people are promiscuous.

53. One friend of mine said, "I had no choice but to be promiscuous—no one ever wanted to see me a second time."

54. Some people are promiscuous because they are looking for a lover.

55. Others are promiscuous because they have already found one.

56. Promiscuity anesthetizes many aches.

57. Promiscuity ups the *ante* with each sexual encounter.

58. Promiscuity is the nightmare of Don Juan.

59. Promiscuity is the quest for what can never be attained.

60. Promiscuity is hope.

61. Promiscuity is a sadness, a rut, a daily self-degradation.

62. Promiscuity is the last true adventure, the last ecstasy, the last *rain forest* of industrial-consumer man.

63. Promiscuity is a means of remaining a perpetual adolescent.

64. Promiscuity is a means of growing up.

65. Promiscuity fails to satisfy that most important need—for intimacy, rootedness, shelter.

66. Promiscuity supplies these in small, ecstatic doses.

67. Promiscuity is a sexual version of chain-smoking.

68. Promiscuity is a sexual version of kneeling in church.

69. Promiscuity is a school of hard knocks, the parent that abuses all its children.

70. Promiscuity gives us something we can acquire no other way: the wisdom of prostitutes.

71. One effect of hiring a hustler, or paying for sex, is the realization afterward that sex is something most people will do with you for *nothing!* One night, after leaving a hustler's apartment in New York, on my way home, I walked through a park filled with men cruising and was startled to realize that all of them would do exactly what had just cost me thirty-five dollars for free.

72. Promiscuity squanders—one has nothing to show for years and years of spent sperm.

73. Promiscuity forms character, builds men.

74. Promiscuity is always planning its next expedition.

75. Promiscuity eventually degenerates into mere habit and, like any habit, is very hard to break.

76. Harder to break than, say, cigarette smoking, because promiscuity is an attempt to escape from loneliness.

77. Promiscuity guarantees loneliness.

78. Many people enjoy promiscuity in their prime and then denounce it in middle age. (Saint Augustine is the most famous of these.)

79. In youth, promiscuity bestows the rapture of poets and saints.

80. In old age, it means haunting the truckstops on I-75.

81. When the author of *Tricks* jokingly told one of his partners, "You know I only like you for your ass," the man replied, in total seriousness, "Yes, I know." (This funny, and sad, exchange sums up the nature of promiscuity.)

82. In a promiscuous world, people come to believe they are worth no more than their genitals.

83. In a promiscuous world, they're right.

84. When Henry James returned to visit America in 1910, he was struck by the great number of New Yorkers eating candy bars. Seventy years later, we were eating each other: the penis as lollipop.

85. It is pointless to feel guilty about promiscuity, so long as you enjoy(ed) it, and harm(ed) no one. One may after all have brought joy into the lives of others and it was, let's face it, a great adventure.

86. Almost everyone disdains promiscuity.

87. Yet all those who think abstinence will be practiced by the majority of people during the age of AIDS—all those who think promiscuity has ceased—are deluded.

88. As King Lear said, "Let copulation thrive; the gilded fly doth lecher in my sight."

89. (As Anthony said of Cleopatra, "She makes hungry where most she satisfies.")

90. It took three or four years for promiscuity to slow down to its present level, after the appearance of AIDS—for a simple reason: Stopping promiscuity was like stopping Niagara Falls.

91. Promiscuity ceases the moment one falls in love.

92. It resumes when that condition fades.

93. Promiscuity was once associated with joy, travel, toothpaste, Brazil, San Juan, Paris, Berlin, hamburgers, automobiles, insurance, poppers, gymnasiums, designer

jeans, designer drugs, Calvin Klein underwear, discotheques, cosmetics, vitamins, clothes, movies, airplanes, subways, men's rooms, piers, Central Park, Land's End, Buena Vista Park, Folsom Street, the West Side Highway, marijuana, cocaine, ethyl chloride, Mexico, the Philippines, Miami, Provincetown, Fire Island, Canal Jeans, Bloomingdale's, the balcony of the Saint, bars, baths, sidewalks, Lisbon, Madrid, Mykonos, certain magazines, four a.m., Stuyvesant Park, the grocery store, the laundromat, autumn, summer, winter, spring, bicycles, T-shirts, and Rice-A-Roni.

92. Not anymore.

Notes on Celibacy

1. THE DICTIONARY DEFINES *celibate* as "unmarried," but it is used—perhaps because of its association with the Catholic priesthood—to mean "not having sex." The word for this is *chaste*. But *chaste* sounds medieval, archaic, demented. So—since once people misuse a word, it is impossible to restore its original meaning—*celibate* it is.

2. Celibacy isn't new. It's been around for eons, a form of asceticism associated with holiness (*asceticism*, from the Greek *asketikos*, from *askein*, "to exercise").

3. Celibacy is a kind of exercise. It's something you consciously adopt, work at, continue, maintain, like a routine for abdominals at the gym. It takes effort.

4. Celibacy has over the centuries been associated with priests. The chief characteristic of priests, Nietzsche wrote, is *resentment*.

5. In recent times, celibacy has been associated with social climbers, interior decorators, art dealers, or people like the late Andy Warhol who feel sex is messy, an energy drain, not worth the trouble, because it interferes with one's career: the pursuit of fame and fortune.

6. Some athletes feel celibacy is essential to peak performance. Some writers think that when a novel is finally underway, they should not have sex because it will only

ruin their concentration, introduce new elements, destroy the state that some of them even call holiness.

7. Celibacy has now been reintroduced into a culture that thought it ridiculous—witness the tumult in the Catholic Church—by the terrors of the plague, because celibacy is the *only* form of safe sex *everyone* agrees is safe.

8. There are two reasons to be celibate: so you will not infect yourself; so you will not infect others.

9. For example, a friend of mine who became celibate four years ago to preserve his own health, a man whose diet, exercise regime, personal life had all been geared toward physical well-being during the oh-so-health-conscious seventies, contracted AIDS last winter and died, astonishing all of his friends. Moral? He perhaps prolonged his own life by not reexposing himself to the virus, but, best of all, and here was his greatness, *he infected no one else.*

10. Celibacy was very difficult even to consider four years ago. It was, you might say, unthinkable. So awful, that the first time the plague became real for me was not when I learned there was a peculiar skin cancer going around that had previously been seen only in Africa, but when a friend of mine who had it was told by his doctor, "You cannot have sex anymore." *This* seemed awful: celibacy.

11. (Five years later, another friend with the same disease was told by his doctor, "You *must* continue to have sex." Safe sex—for his mental and emotional health. 1987 versus 1982.)

12. The first celibate I knew was a friend who decided just when the plague appeared to stop having sex. At that time, I thought him cold, unfeeling, puritanical, neurotic: a man who turned celibate, I thought, far too easily. Later I concluded he was simply more intelligent and disciplined than the rest of us. He became outwardly more calm; he left his gym, changed his friends, habits, went to school,

became obsessed with a vegetarian diet, and then, three years later, tried to kill himself. Celibacy is tough.
13. Celibacy isolates the celibate. It leaves certain urges and needs unanswered. Two women on *This Week with David Brinkley* were arguing condoms one Sunday morning. One woman said there is no such thing as safe sex— argued that abstinence, total abstinence, was the only sane course to follow and said giving up sex was no harder than giving up cigarettes. The other woman retorted, "Giving up sex is *not* like giving up cigarettes. Sex is a far, far deeper need than the desire for a cigarette." I agree (even though the seventies turned sex into chain-smoking).
14. Celibacy alters one's relationship to the world.
15. On the plus side, it eliminates anxiety. You can't worry about the sex you're not having. The sex you are not having cannot cause remorse, sleepless nights, anger, fear, or loathing.
16. Celibacy produces a certain calm, at first, a little like the calm you felt when, in the seventies, you had to stop having sex—Time out!—because you were taking medicine to eliminate amoebas or gonorrhea. You could relax. You have more time to yourself; you stay home, you read, eat, write letters, watch TV, make meals in advance, use the Tupperware that's been gathering dust for years on a high shelf, walk down the street with a sense of quiet, go to bed early. You do not find yourself far from home at ridiculous hours, in dark places. You cool out.
17. Celibacy is benign, detached. (The man on the prowl was avaricious, alert, on edge.)
18. Celibacy is something you can be proud of, like a savings account passbook, like the number of days an alcoholic has been sober. You are finally doing the right thing.
19. Celibacy makes sex ideal. When you are not having

sex—with its mess, its egotism, pettiness, degradation, risk, self-love—you think of it in the imagination. The sex you have in your imagination is always sex just as you want it; one even does things, in imagined sex, one would not/could not do in real life, especially now. Sex becomes an ideal you look forward to, like happiness or God.

20. Celibacy makes the world *more* erotic, not less. (Celibacy is a dam that makes a fast-running, tempestuous, deep river overflow its banks and cover the earth as a calm, shallow lake. It bathes everything you see—people of all ages, stores, groceries late at night, streets, houses with lighted lamps, the change of seasons. The whole world seems erotic to you because you are not having sex, or encountering it in limited, specific, disillusioning places.)

21. Celibacy, like any habit, reinforces itself: the longer you are celibate, the easier it is, the less you want sex.

22. Or so it seems. On the negative side of celibacy: Celibacy is in fact stressful, and arduous, because it closes off an avenue by which we enter the human community. Celibacy leaves you feeling apart.

23. Celibacy leaves you standing in the yard alone on a moonlit night, looking up at the stars, wondering: *What is the beauty of this night for?* (One friend of mine in London walked into a park and hugged a *tree*.)

24. Celibacy is curiously deflating; it takes the craziness out of life, it makes people less . . . than they were before.

25. Celibacy leaves you wondering what you will do with the rest of your life.

26. Celibacy leaves you wondering whether there is any point in going to: Amsterdam, Berlin, Spain, or Brazil. Celibacy makes you ask yourself, *Is it worth going to Madrid just for the Prado?* Or, *Should I go to London and just go to museums?*

27. Celibacy leaves you wondering if you should marry a woman. (But how?)

28. Celibacy leaves you with your chief goal an intimate relationship with another man whom you can spend the rest of your life with. (But how?)

29. Celibacy is prideful: The celibate thinks himself smarter, more disciplined than fools who go on having sex while a plague is underway. Celibates feel a certain contempt for those weaker souls.

30. Celibacy engenders anger. Nietzsche was right. Whether they know it or not, celibates feel deprived and denied, like children whose mother has not given them a good-night kiss (which is what we might say sex is, or what Proust said sex was: one version of a mother's good-night kiss).

31. Celibacy changes you—like living alone for a long time and getting used to it. When you go back to the world, you are no longer the same person. You regard sex from a distance, a new perspective; you see it objectively, which is both good *and* bad.

32. Celibacy turns some amusing friends into people who seem to have had a lobotomy.

33. Celibacy leaves you with a whole lot of time to fill.

34. Celibacy makes you realize that almost everything you did before was centered on the pursuit of sex.

35. Celibacy makes you feel like a toilet seat in a motel room with one of those paper bands that proclaims that the seat has not been sat on since the motel maid cleaned and disinfected it—or at least that's how I felt whenever I left the public clinic on Ninth Avenue in the seventies, after the doctor had told me I was "cured" of amoebiasis. What to do with a sanitary band was the question then. And it is, now.

36. Celibacy ignores the lesson taught me by a man I went home with from the Jewel, a porn theater in New York, a year ago: "The skin," he explained in a cab going north, "needs to be touched."

37. (Later he told me he was the founder of Sexual Compulsives Anonymous, a group modeled on AA for people who tricked helplessly. After talking about this and undressing, we ended up not having sex at all, and I left, crestfallen—proving that we really do need sex, from time to time, and the skin needs more than a touch.)

38. Celibacy brings you in line with the teachings of the Catholic Church: You are homosexual, but you do not perform any homosexual acts. (This may seem a contradiction to some, and perfectly logical to others.)

39. Celibacy makes you fear even safe sex because even safe sex can "intoxicate" and lead to unsafe sex. (All sex starts the same way.)

40. Celibacy makes even dancing dubious, because although dancing is still a superb sublimation of sex, six hours with other shirtless men and good music leaves you wanting sex when you walk home.

41. Celibacy makes you realize there are what the Church calls "occasions of sin"—that is, places, situations that you should avoid because they weaken the will, the resolve not to have sex.

42. Celibacy is easier in the country than in town for the same reason it's easier not to eat chocolate-chip cookies if you don't have them around the house.

43. Celibacy is easier, no matter where you live, if you swim, go for walks, or exercise. Going to a gym, on the other hand, in which muscular athletes undress in the locker room beside you may make celibacy more difficult.

44. Celibacy is easiest when you have other sources of ego satisfaction, and human interaction, in your life—work, for example, or taking care of someone. Celibates may become workaholics because there is nothing else to do with the energy. Celibacy means we are going to have a lot more books, novels, screenplays, et cetera, because writers who are not having sex might as well work.

45. If, as the late Arthur Bell said, AIDS was caused by piano bars, celibacy may well be responsible for the boom in gay theater. If you can't go to the baths or pick people up in bars, but still want to go out, what's left? A play.

46. Celibacy isn't funny—it should be, like safe sex, but it isn't. It's depressing.

47. Celibacy—with no foreseeable end—cuts off hope. It seems like a death sentence, which is ironic, since it is adopted to evade exactly that.

48. Celibacy has no awards dinner. Yet celibacy is like saving stamps—you feel there should be something you can turn it in for. But the only reward you want—sex—is not available, and so the celibate feels even more unrewarded for his sacrifice. Health—the greatest possession of all, the "prize" for being celibate—is not a reward people think of in positive terms; it is simply the absence of sickness. And the celibate ends up asking bitterly, "What is health *for?*"

49. Celibacy is deceptive because sexual desire is only a river that has gone momentarily underground, but not ceased to exist; it may surface at any time and take you right over the falls.

50. Celibacy is dangerous because it is an extreme, and therefore leads to an opposite extreme: When the celibate breaks down and has sex, it tends to be orgiastic—a release from all his days of denial. `

51. Celibacy is deeply depressing and should be recognized as such. The only thing more depressing is the remorse after violating it unwisely.

52. Celibacy is bad for the hair and skin. (Unless we view it in the larger context of what AIDS does to the hair and skin.)

53. Celibacy may induce a feeling of virtue in homosexuals who have had trouble reconciling their sex life and spiritual goals.

54. Celibacy is going to have profound effects on American life—from fashion to foreign policy. How do you dress when you don't want to attract people? How to keep society from going to war, when it's not having sex?

55. The Catholic Church considers celibacy a gift.

56. Celibacy is not for the average slob—celibacy is for the few: the frightened, the disciplined, the intelligent. Far wiser, perhaps, the person who concedes the power of sexual needs by providing for them in as "safe" a way as possible and avoids the isolation and despair celibacy can induce. As a friend said, "Everyone needs to be hugged." Yet even this is not easy—it wasn't before, and it isn't now.

57. Celibacy is most easily practiced when life is on an even keel. Deep depression and extreme happiness both produce sexual desire: the first for solace, the second for celebration.

58. Celibacy is an art.

59. Celibacy is a discipline.

60. Celibacy is an expression of temperament—a psychological response to facts that produce in others of different temperament a different reaction. Celibacy is as irrational as it is rational a choice.

61. Celibacy may have as much to do with the climate of sadness produced by this disease as it does with common sense. Everyone is depressed.

62. "Why couldn't you find another person," I asked a friend who thinks about these things at lunch one day, "take the test, and, if you're both negative, go off together and do absolutely everything you want to?" "Because," he said, "that's like asking why two Jews in the thirties could not have gone off to the country and led normal lives while their friends were all being taken to the ovens. Sex isn't just physical—it's cultural, too." I thought about this all the way home, and he may be right.

63. Celibacy is an expression of guilt.

64. Celibacy is an expression of the will to live—the only rational response to a world in which, if the doctors are correct, millions are infected and only a fraction of them know it.

65. Celibacy is sanity.

66. Celibacy is madness.

67. Celibacy is the future.

Beauty NOW

Beauty NOW. Hair, Eyes, Lips, Makeup, Fashion NOW. NEW ICONS. What Everyone's Talking About: Books, Plays, Music, Food, Travel, Makeup, Eskimos, Chess, Virgins.

"SOMETIMES IN LIFE," someone marvelously French said (oh, all right! *Proust*), "all we need is a change of weather." Well darling, its PUMPKIN-Time in the Big MANGO. *Mejor dicho:* Autumn in New York. Why does it set the heart *dancing?* Because we're back in town after a long, slow, DEFENSIVE vacation at the beach and WE FEEL GOOD ABOUT OURSELVES. (Not to mention how good we LOOK). Time to take stock. To choose what in the new fall season is right FOR US. To strengthen Beauty Points: Attitude, Hair, Eyes, Lips, Skin, Makeup, Knees, Body. Time for buckling down with all that is best in WHAT'S NEW: A NEW diet, a NEW kind of Romance, a NEW You. What's NEW in what WE SEE for YOU this FALL '85—the BEST fall of your lives—begins with:

Beauty NOW. A NEW APPROACH. Those long, pensive walks you took on Fire Island, Laguna Beach, or Cape Cod in late August have PAID OFF. Those lonely nights midweek when your house was empty, and instead of doing something risky like visiting the RACK you lay on the deck listening to a Vivaldi guitar concerto, wondering "What's a flower for?" are yielding BIG DIVIDENDS: People see you're at your PEAK OF BEAUTY. Of course, you *used* to stop and chat with these adoring FANS, but this fall you have a reserved and distant and MYSTERIOUS air. People wonder WHY you're not cruising them. Why you don't LOCK EYES ON THE STREET. *You* know the reason. It's simple. YOU'RE SCARED. At your job—which will be, this fall, MUCH more absorbing, fulfilling, and interesting than it has EVER been before (and you know why), you keep that GUARDED, yet OPEN feeling as you mix with all the DIVINE FLESH that congregates in our city.

IMAGE: A cold and silver SEA seen from the stone cell of an IRISH MONK in the sixth century, transcribing a text of Aristotle in the most BEAUTIFUL CALLIGRA-PHY the world has ever known. YOU: a secret, wild rose growing on a misty, cool, high promontory outside his window—even though you're in the middle of perhaps the most HYSTERICAL city in the world, or even (who knows) some little speedtrap down SOUTH (which has its OWN hysteria). Beauty NOW is CALM. Beauty NOW is HEALTH. The NEW ICONS are: Virgins, Stone Age Tribes, ES-KIMOS, Sophomores in Town on a Class Trip, Any-body from North Dakota, Chinese chess champions with BRACES. The OLD ICONS—hot men, used men, Italian baggage handlers, Puerto Rican messengers. Syrian taxi drivers, dark, mustached men in their prime—are OUT OUT OUT. *Don't touch!* Glance at them MAYBE on the windows of airline offices as you walk by on this CRISP, FALL AFTERNOON, *not* directly. (They won't look back anyway, since everyone is practicing the NEW RESERVE.) BONUS: Glancing at the plate glass window of the AVIANCA office lets you see your—

Hair NOW. Hair NOW is of course short on the sides, thick on top, though you could break away from the pack by growing an AFRO now. (*Live.*) Hair NOW, in whatever style *you* choose to present it, is, of course, HEALTH-HAIR. Remember your FOCUS in Fall '85: Carrots, raw greens and other vitamin-A-rich foods FEED Follicles. DANGER: If some evening your haircut is INCRED-

IBLE—SO GOOD you must go out, then do it, but simply to SHOW YOUR HAIRCUT. The theme for Fall '85? *Look But Do Not Touch.* (Remember Mom when her hair and nails were *Just Right* before going out?) Try taking your FABULOUS HAIRCUT to SAFE locations like: The Guggenheim, Saint Patrick's, your favorite J.O. Club. (And *remember*, at the latter, there is no outfit on earth more DEVASTATING than simple white Jockey shorts and T-shirt. DESIGNER LABELS: *VERBOTEN.*) Or take your haircut out for a WALK. Wherever you are, remember: Hair NOW is about being STRESS-FREE, and INNER PEACE comes from knowing you are ALIVE and committed to REMAINING SO in the near term. Health-Hair NOW is the expression of that commitment, and so, darling are—

Lips NOW. Lips *used* to be for: Sucking, Licking, Hissing, Talking Dirty, Slurping. Now they're for: Discussing the Meaning of Existence, Prayer, and Song. Lips NOW have never looked more FABULOUS because they are PRISTINE. Join the *Gay Men's Chorus!* Gargle regularly with warm water, baking soda, and/or salt, to keep the edges and inner lining of the mouth MOIST and RED. Don't GNAW at your lower lip even though the New Reserve may induce TENSION. Remember your FOCUS: Lips are COMPOSED, SERENE, yet GENEROUS. Lips '85 convey a WEALTH OF EXPERIENCE, AND a wealth of WISDOM. Lips '85 send a message: NO. *We are no longer doing certain things.* This can be HARD ON LIPS. LIPS '85 are used to saying, "I DON'T DO THAT NOW. Because SOMEONE PISSED IN THE POOL, darling! Because we all realize now that anonymous (Let-Yourself-GO) sex is OUT, unless you want to spend this FALL '85 petrified over every pimple and cold sore and ache. Lips '85 want to know: What about Safe SEX? SAFE SEX can be FABOU for the lips—if they don't have to EXPLAIN IT to the person first. Whose lips enjoy NEGOTIATING rules of lovemaking before sex? KEY: Look for people ON YOUR LEVEL: AWARE, WITH IT, KNOWING, ON THE CREST OF THE WAVE. If you should see a HUMPY ANGEL you *cannot* pass up, use your LIPS '85 to find OUT what he knows. And if he doesn't know ENOUGH (and LIPS '85 are all about KNOWING. Why else do you live in the most fabulous city in the world?), then simply give him the telephone number of a FRIEND who will explain on your behalf Condoms, Hydrogen Peroxide, Clorox, Oxynol-9 (and let's not kid ourselves any longer about Kissing: I know this is tough on die-hard romantics, but grow up.) Sally Slut says to herself, "If I have to go over there and raise the issue of DEATH with that gorgeous man, I'd rather not bother." (Makes sense, Sally.) *Suzy Sensible makes the effort.* Both ask, "What IS sex, anyway?" Or (more accurately) "What WAS sex?"—before going ahead with it. Use Lips to redefine, RETHINK what same-sex desire is *really* all about. Use Lips to sing fabulous, sophisticated, bluesy RODGERS & HART ballads that still express JUST HOW WE FEEL. CONSIDER: Taking your FABULOUS NEW LIPS to church. Lips '85 look great in a PEW because PRAYING and FOLLOWING THE LITURGY are SAFE SEX. BONUS: At the coffee hours after the service at Dignity or the gay synagogue, you may meet men who are there for something other than INSTANT oral gratification. Use your Lips to discuss THE SOUL. (You HAVE one, darling. You just MISPLACED it during the seventies! It's someplace around the apartment. LOOK FOR IT.) And while you do, practice FACIAL ISOMETRICS. Because Lips '85 are both PHYSICAL and SPIRITUAL Lips, CENTERED, CALM, COMPOSED Lips, and so, darling, are—

Eyes NOW. Eyes this fall are VERY IMPORTANT, more important than ever before, more important than LIPS, because they are—quite frankly—our CHIEF SEXUAL ORGAN this season. BE CREATIVE. Take mental photographs of HOT, HUMPY MEN all over town to be developed later in the silence of your own bedroom where you will be having SAFE SEX with yourself. (The body simply does not like foreign sperm.) The hot, humpy PUERTO RICAN MESSENGER hanging onto the subway strap next to yours? DEVOUR HIM WITH YOUR EYES. FOCUS on a LIMB, a BUTTOCK, the shadow of a beard on his square jaw, a muscle flickering beneath the skin. (HOT STUFF, darling.) You CAN have sex with *les yeux*. (See Wordsworth, "The Daffodils." Or Cavafy, the DIVINE Alexandrian poet who had sex simply by EXAMINING fabrics with a cute salesman behind the counter. BE CREATIVE.) Whether you RUN, or do TAI CHI, or SWIM, take in the sight of SWEATY ATHLETES in their UNSPEAKABLE BEAUTY—the stain that a perspiring ass makes on PALE GRAY SWEATPANTS, the way HAIR clings to the forehead of someone who has spent SIX HOURS playing BASKETBALL—as you USE SPORTS to SMOOTH YOURSELF OUT during this period when oral satisfaction is being denied. (*Type A personalities especially:* Take thirty-minute SWIMS three times a week. Use goggles to protect your eyes. Do not take too long in the shower. Be careful not to *slip* in the shower, because the floors of many gym shower rooms these days are *covered* with spermatozoa.) SUGGESTION: Get into the pool in the lane next to someone CUTE. Make your FLIP-TURN when HE does, so you end up *face-to-crotch* with his *Speedo* underwater! OR: Swim the CRAWL slightly *behind* him, so you can see his ass tighten and relax with his flutter kick, and the flare of his back, and those beautiful chests coming toward you in the other lanes. Because—

EYES '85 are all about PERIPHERAL VISION. They are HONEST, FORTHRIGHT, WARM, but CLOSED.

Consider going to the GYM at odd hours, if the visual stimuli of rush hour overload the circuits. Go LATE when the gym is nearly EMPTY and you do not have to worry about being caught STARING directly at other weight lifters, or TRIPPING on the track as you run looking down at the SEXPOT punching the bag beneath you on the gym floor. CHANGE gyms if yours produces an urge to visit the Baths. Visit the BATHS if VERY FIRM about Safe Sex (this is only for advanced students) for visual feasts of gorgeous homosexuals DENYING DEATH. Less Advanced: Take architectural walking tours of the city—at odd hours; avoid cruisy parks. HOP A TRAIN Up the Hudson to see AUTUMN. (Now that you are still alive, life has never seemed so *precious* to you, and all its extraordinary beauty.) Use the energy left over from NOT HAVING SEX to EXERCISE your eyes by: Paying bills on time, *devouring* the letters of: Proust, Henry, William, Alice James, Thomas Mann, Bernard Shaw, Bismarck, Goethe. Finish Robert Musil's *The Man Without Qualities*. WRITE a five-act opera based on same. Watch the man in the building behind yours undress at night. Get to know the PORN you stored years ago under the bed. EXPAND your CONCEPT OF PORN by finding nearly everything you see EROTIC. (The New Celibates know all about this FABULOUS BONUS.) Jerk off with a small mirror on the shelf opposite the toilet seat to show JUST YOUR HAND on your genitals. AVOID PIG EYES on the street. Remember—if America were an Islamic Republic (and more and more people are thinking it SHOULD BE), you might be wearing CHADORS, leaving ONLY the eyes (barely) exposed, which is what EYES '85 are ALL ABOUT. OR: Use your FABULOUS, EDUCATED EYES to make your apartment PRISSY—use enough period furniture, porcelain, ormolu to make a penis THINK TWICE before getting hard; *or* create a space TOO EMBARRASSING to ask another hu-

man being back to: Village NIGHTMARE! *Or:* If TER-
RIBLY SECURE in the New Restraint, make your room
IRRESISTIBLE for those evenings you'll be asking friends
over to discuss History: *Sex in the Seventies,* or the latest
kiss-and-tell biography of Tennessee Williams, because
NOW THAT NO ONE IS MAKING LOVE TO YOU,
you need the emotional BONDS *friends* provide more than
ever, *and* books about Other People's Sex Lives. When you
MUST GET OUT, go to the Eagle and LOOK at other
men. (Remembering the rule this season is: *Mira Pero No
Toques.*) (Has anything at the Eagle REALLY changed?)
WATCH the new plays, films, cabaret that always EX-
PLODE between now and the holidays. CHOOSE the J.O.
Club that is right for YOU. Is DANCING your perfect Sex
Substitute? Then OGLE the HOT, HANDSOME, PUMPED-
UP GYM BODIES, PERFECT DELTOIDS in a sweaty
discotheque. If this leads to the balcony, STAY HOME.
(There are people fresh out of the hospital up there.) SUGGES-
TION: Spend Saturday NIGHT parked in front of your
TV. Look for: Diet Soda commercials—*pornographic!*—or
the obligatory scene by the pool in *Love Boat,* with humpy
L.A. extras parading in the background. *(Danger:* Don't
watch the scene the Main Actors are playing—this may
bring your T-cell count DOWN.) Try reading CYNTHIA
OZICK. Or—better yet—use the mirror in your bathroom
to perfect your—
Makeup NOW. *Incredible. Revolutionary. Unheard of.* Industry types will tell you this year's eyeliner and blush are
based on smoky, woodsy, fall colors, but we are under too
much pressure, personally and historically, to put out that
line of shit. Smoky, woodsy colors, darling, are NOT In.
Nor are pastels, peaches, or the injection of *sheep placenta
from Bulgaria.* BE HONEST. In the old days weren't we
the first to shatter *oppressive Makeup Myth* by telling you,
quite simply, there is no chemical in all of Estée Lauder,

Max Factor, OR Clinique's bottomless vats to compare with the GLOW a really marvelous, time-consuming, no-holds-barred, midafternoon *you-know-what* could give you (and WASN'T IT, once-in-a-lifetime, the TRUTH?) *That's all over now!* Makeup '85 is the VERY LITTLE SEX glow. The SAFE SEX, or NO SEX, glow is slightly different—it can even look a bit DEAD—but not to worry. With all the chlorine from the pool you'll be doing thirty miles of LAPS in this fall each month to CALM DOWN, you will look POSITIVELY ETHEREAL. Be DECISIVE. DUMP the Queen Helene Face Mask, the cucumber facial, the superfatted soap in the TRASH. WE ARE TALKING CLEAR, UNOBSTRUCTED YOU. We are talking the AL-MOST NO SEX glow. Makeup NOW is totally REALIS-TIC. HONEST. SENSIBLE. Discipline is STRICT, faces are held ABOVE the steaming collard greens while your pores say: *Bonjour*, vitamin A! Put your *putz* RIGHT INTO the bouillabaisse, no matter how fashionable the restaurant! Bee Pollen? MAINLINE IT! SUGGESTION: Put a little sign above the bathroom mirror that says: 1. I will wash my face every night. 2. I will not let anyone sit on it. The first involves: Distilled water, a Neutral Soap, at least TWENTY RINSES before patting dry with a CLEAN TOWEL. The second involves GOING STRAIGHT TO BED, where you will be getting lots of GOOD, SOLID SLEEP this Fall because SUPERB SLEEP is ESSENTIAL to your—

Body NOW. Demands getting to KNOW YOUR BODY. And who knows it better than you? *For starters:* KNEES are in wonderful shape, because you're not ON THEM anymore, and you're careful when you RUN to do it on indoor tracks and not that hard, cement sidewalk. BUT-TOCKS are firm because you're exercising on a regular basis. The ASSHOLE is tight, and free of VENEREAL WARTS. In fact, you've NEVER BEEN IN BETTER

SHAPE. Some of you have CHOSEN TO BE FAT, because FAT looks HEALTHY. Others have kept your TEENSY WAIST. You're working out now BECAUSE YOU ENJOY IT. Because EVEN WHEN WE STOP HAVING PICK-UP SEX, we remain as *vain* and *eroticized* as ever! FEET Now are in top condition, and used only in J.O. scenes, or on brisk walks through the woods overlooking the Hudson. BONUS: Massage your feet at home—SENSUOUS and STRESS-DISSOLVING. BONUS: Take your feet on a hiking tour of the Catskills. (But NOT Copacabana Beach or the streets of Paris. Travel is part of Feet NOW but not SEX VACATION—because some diseased QUEEN less ethical than you has been there already and infected the locals!) STOMACHS—unless you've decided to become a Porker—are WASHBOARD. NIPPLES are SUBDUED. GENITALS—bleached in Clorox—are worn UNOBTRU-SIVELY. The INSIDE OF YOUR RECTUM, in fact the entire LOWER COLON, reflects your decision to maintain SPATIAL INTEGRITY. They have also been helped by your emphasis on *whole-grain* cereals mixed with the RAW OATS found in those *divine* bins at your favorite health food store. (STOOLS *float* on the surface because you are eating sufficient roughage.) CONSIDER: Macrobiotic. BONUS: Claims are made it can *bring your T-cell count back to normal.* FACT: You love CHOCOLATE CAKE. (And CHOCOLATE is more important than ever this fall because you have nixed certain other forms of *oral gratification.*) BASIC: Whichever way you go, foundation *must be* a BALANCED, NATURAL DIET of fresh fruit and raw veggies. KEY: FART FOOD is GOOD FOOD because people who fart unpredictably, and often, are *not* going to risk the HUMILIATION entailed in blowing several hundred cubic feet of STALE GAS during a *let-yourself-go* orgasm. They STAY HOME MORE where they can fart to their heart's content! Use this EXTRA TIME to do KNEE

EXERCISES—like *genuflection.* Memorize: "My Body Is the Temple of the Holy Ghost." *Keep it Clean.* With knees, feet, asshole, stomach in PERFECT SHAPE, your body HUMS, and a perfectly working BODY has always been, and is again this fall, the most important, crucial, fundamental element in—

Fashion NOW. Fashion, dressing, because of your totally new situation, *no longer present problems.* BONUS: Kiss good-bye hours wasted in your INSECURE SEX YEARS trying on T-shirts. (As if there was a *magic* T-shirt! As if there was a Mister Right!) The *despair* you felt after a night in the bars when you realized your outfit was NOT WORK-ING! Those DEGRADING afternoons spent with people MUCH younger than you in CANAL JEANS looking for pants that showed your ASS off! Your ASS *is in great shape, darling,* because it's WART-FREE! (For the longest time *ever.*) In Fall '85, you are not dressing to show your Body off. (Unless you're a sadist; and that's for ANOTHER COLUMN, dear.) You are dressing to be APPROPRIATE, UNNOTICED, COMFORTABLE, RELAXED. So BE CREATIVE. Fashion NOW is revolutionary because it no longer has to be validated by someone *unzipping his pants.* WHY? Because you're off FAST-FOOD SEX. It was thrill-ing, *of course.* But it wasn't doing your BODY any good. Junk food never does, darling. And it's FABULOUS now to know you won't be down on your KNEES over the next bimbo who walks through the door. Think of this Fall as a SEX BREAK. Think of the *New Celibacy* as a *Holiday,* a *Moment for Reflection.* Use this OPPORTUNITY to re-trench, rededicate yourself to Old Ideals (which are JUST LIKE Old Clothes, darling: You can always pull them out of storage TEN YEARS LATER because EVERYTHING ALWAYS comes back! Look at NEW WAVE!) Use your OLD IDEALS to get out OF TOWN, close to NATURE, read the DIVINE COMEDY, listen to ALL OF BARTOK

straight through! Start writing that long-lost cousin in San-
dusky, Ohio, who goes to church twice a week, is an aide
in a nursing home, lifts weights, and has never even been
SUNBURNED! Learn how to be a SUPERB *voyeur.* Or—
if you know you'll never be able to DO WITHOUT
indefinitely—come to grips with the NEW REALITY. Buy
a package of LUXURIOUS CONDOMS and become familiar with them at home. Then INVITE FRIENDS over
and give each one of *them* a package. DISCUSS your feelings about the Icky things (the Only Way you'll be able to
have ANY SEX AT ALL in the coming years, dear) as you
pass them around the table. (Blow them up to wear as
party hats.) PARTY GAME: Try putting them on in record
time. (Winner gets two tickets to *Cats.*) Learn to overcome
your distaste, embarrasment, shyness, and hesitation about
using them, or even SUGGESTING they be used to a prospective husband. Remember, darling, YOU HAVE NO
CHOICE. It's raincoats or *nothing* so long as the skies are
POURING DOWN VIRUSES. Be SMART. BEHAVE, dear
heart. Use this *incredible* time to develop your—

Attitude NOW. *What people are reading, seeing, talking about.*
The Chinese are going ahead with the FOUR MODERN-
IZATIONS, darling, and SO MUST WE. This fall you're
WATCHFUL, WORRIED, HOPEFUL, SAD, REALISTIC,
DEPRESSED, TENSE, CALM, ANXIOUS, ELATED, AP-
PREHENSIVE, DETERMINED, BURSTING WITH EN-
ERGY AND AFRAID TO USE IT. Let's face it: You're
CONFUSED. You've never been so BESET with CON-
TRADICTORY MESSAGES. You want to be CALM but
you're really NERVOUS. You want to be COMPOSED but
you're actually UPSET. You've never felt SO ALIVE and
never before been so CONSCIOUS OF THE PERILS in-
volved in LIFE. You live in a culture SATURATED with
COME-ONS, a society that PUTS A PREMIUM ON BEING
ATTRACTIVE, but there is cancer in the air! You move

through a city where you'd like to sleep with TEN MEN on every block, but you just don't know *which ones* are LETHAL. You're told by one set to make your body DROP DEAD, and by another NOT TO USE IT for any of those things that relieve our awful SOLITUDE. If years ago you were alienated from the world because of your homosexuality, NOW you're alienated from *homosexuality!* Some are understandably in a state of HIBERNATION. You're looking for a MIDDLE ROAD. The way we see it: The Oil Glut ended, and so has the SEX GLUT. And *you're* left with the hangover. But you know we recovered from ENERGY CRISIS and we can get through the LOVE CATASTROPHE. What to do? Press your HOLD Button. You know the NEW SOBRIETY, darling, can be a FABULOUS OPPORTUNITY. To ask just what IS going on. And how you want the FUTURE to be. Form small groups of CLOSE FRIENDS for Discussion and Consciousness-Enrichment. (Divine Henry James said, "Consciousness is everything." Isn't it, just.) BE REALISTIC. Ask yourself, *What would happen if the plague stopped tomorrow?* If the folks who brought us Pearl Harbor and the SONY Walkman found a cure *Tuesday?* BE HONEST: Everyone would start *slurping* again. (*Our Mouths, Ourselves.*) The gay newspapers you've been reading faithfully since this started would fill up with articles on BUTT-PLUGS. People would start getting *snotty* again about rejection and selection. *It wouldn't take much for us all to become junkies again!* But you're *aware* of that. *And too smart to let it happen!* You want to use this time to change your WHOLE APPROACH. Because, darling, when the plague ends—whenever!—and the papers DO drag out those *in-depth* features on Art Nouveau cockrings, and the man blows his whistle and yells, "*Que la fête commence!*", we want you to be just a LITTLE DIFFERENT. *Isn't that what being GAY is all about?* And until that happens—if the detail, *detail*, DETAIL of these endless precautions is just too much for you—then THINK BIG as you make your plans to get through this. Call the Whitney Museum, *ask for the Director*—don't be intimidated by Authority!—and tell him you'd like him to commission CHRISTO (the artist who put sheets all over those TINY islands in Biscayne Bay, and WANTED to do the paths in Central Park) to WRAP YOU. That, darling, will solve everything and make *you* WHAT PEOPLE ARE TALKING ABOUT this fall—the *best*, most *exciting*, and *terrifying* fall of your lives! Autumn in New York! Why does it set the heart DANCING? Because this year, my darlings, you are living on the EDGE. And we want you to maintain your BALANCE.

Next month: SHOPPING.

My Last Trick

HE WORE A BLACK T-shirt and faded jeans and he was not so good-looking he was threatening, but good-looking enough to resemble dessert. He had large blue-gray eyes and a shock of dirty-blond hair falling down his forehead and a mustache (conveniently) of the same color, and he was stalking. He was the person who comes into the bar who wants to leave it in five minutes, if he can, with a trick. He was shorter than I—always a plus—and this added to the impression that he was swimming through the shallows, somewhere at crotch level, like a shark with one thought and one thought only: food. Everyone at the bar was engrossed in a television movie, but the young man—who could have been anywhere from twenty-five to twenty-nine (the golden age of Trick)—kept moving in and out of the bar's two rooms, and the garden outside, not looking at the television, searching for companionship. His eyes, when they came into the light of the doorway and caught mine, were those pale, clear, luminous slates on which anything might be written; the eyes of the Trick that say, "I am nobody. Who are you?" The tablets we played with as children—on which we could draw something and, by picking up the cellophane sheet, erase it instantly and return the tablet to a pale gray blank—are what he was, are what the Trick is. *Write on me,* he says, and then lift the cellophane and I'll be ready for another to draw *his* picture on me. This expression gives nothing away because (a) there is nothing to give away; and (b) he doesn't want to limit himself to a particular role, because if he does that, he reduces the number of potential tricks, and tonight he can't take chances, tonight he must get laid.

When a man comes into a bar in that mood—so horny, as a friend of mine once said, your ass squeaks when you walk and you think as you're strolling Fifth Avenue or the aisles at Bloomingdale's that people can hear the noise your buttocks are making in their extreme longing—he often scares the horses. It is possible to be too horny. I watched him follow a short, plump, smoldering marshmallow into the garden—another man clearly on the prowl—but he got nowhere and returned to the bar. Then a battered, older man with liquid blue eyes entered, and the black T-shirt nodded at him, and I felt the curious deflation of knowing that he would sleep with any one of us, that whoever said yes first could have him. I totaled things up. On the plus side: If he were that horny, if he were demented, ready to leave with three physically dissimilar men, he would surely be gone, body-devouring sex. On the minus: he was a cheap slut. Seated on a barrel in the corner while he passed back and forth like Lady Macbeth sleepwalking, or the ball of string we dangled in front of the cat to get her to grab at it with a paw, I didn't move. I couldn't. I had a cold coming on, I was low, I had come to the point where I no longer spoke Trick. I'd had—a month before—my last dark stranger.

I hesitate to call him My Last Trick because I learned early in life never to say, stamping my foot in anger, "I will *never* come to this bar again!" Or, "That is the *last* time I set foot on Fire Island." Or, "This is quite simply the *last* time I *ever* go to the baths." I knew even then the words never and *last* had a magic power. To say you'd never return to the Eagle meant you were there the following

Saturday. To say this visit to Fire Island was your last was to wonder, as the boat returned to Sayville, whom you could visit next time. To promise you would never pass beneath the arch of the Everard again meant you were there the next night. *Never, last time, that's it* were shibboleths as potent as *open, sesame.* The only time you give something up is the time you are so indifferent to it you don't even make the vow or use the word *never.* You simply forget to do it. The last time we do things in life, we are not aware till years later that it was: the last time we saw Bob, the last time we visited London, the last time we waterskied; years pass and then one day we realize: I've never been back, and probably won't, so that was, though I didn't know it, my last time.

There were nights, of course, I wondered—would there come a time when I'd see someone out the door, turn to the cat, and say, "All right. THAT was my last trick. I'm stopping—with number one thousand four hundred forty-four!" Or wake him up the next day, or say to him just before he left, "By the way, you are my last trick," and present him with an old toaster or an alarm clock? And my friend, when I opened the door, would ask, "Who was that on the stairs?" And I'd say, "That was my last trick."

"You mean your most recent," he'd say.

"No, the last one I'm *ever* going to have."

He'd look at me, sit down, and light a cigarette.

"I've just decided there's no point," I'd say. "I'm not meeting anyone interesting anymore—I'm not falling in love. I'm just tricking, with people I'll never see again. That was my last."

He'd guffaw.

"I'm *serious!*" I'd say. "Tricking used to be rare and wonderful, but now the market is flooded and it isn't much fun. Remember when only a few people tricked? Well now everyone does it. Tricking caught on. Most tricks—most

people, let's face it—are dull. Or worse, so used to tricking
by now, they're all professional tramps. It used to be something you did to find love, but now it's something you do
because you go to a gym and must be getting in shape for
*some*thing. That was my last trick."

But just then there was a knock on the door. I reached
over and opened it: It was my last trick holding the toaster.
"I'm sorry," he said, "but I just couldn't leave the building
without knowing. What did I do that made you decide to
never trick again?" "Nothing," I said. "You were fine. Really.
You were a good trick. I can't think of a thing wrong." I
took a deep breath and said: "It's just that we didn't—
connect."

"You mean—?"

"Nothing passed between us, there was no—emotion."

"There was excitement!" he said. "You moaned."

"There was excitement, but no emotion," I said. "There
was no—feeling. There was not even any—limerence. We
did not even have a crush on each other."

My friend, seated as near the kitchen door as I, suddenly
kicked his foot out and slammed the door in his face. I
was horrified. "You don't treat people that way!" I screamed.
"He wasn't people," he said, "he was a trick." I opened the
door to apologize, but there was no one there. I went out
into the hall and called—not his name, because I wasn't
sure what it was, but "Come back!" The clatter of his feet
going downstairs, and the slam of the door to the street,
preceded me by two landings all the way down. I considered running out after him, but had to consider the fact
that in a crowd—especially in the ghetto—he would look
like a lot of other people. By the time I reached the fifth
floor again, I was panting and even more angry with my
friend. "You are precisely the problem!" I yelled when I
sat down across the kitchen table from him. My friend said
impatiently, "He was just going to stand there and dither.

You answered his question, what more could you say? He was obviously bad sex."

"Why do you say that?" I said.

"Well, why else wouldn't you see him again?"

"I just explained why," I said.

"Then we're back where we started," he said.

"That was my last trick," I said.

"But what will you *do*?" he said. "How will you live?"

"If I stop tricking?" I said. I paused. "Actually, I don't really know. I don't know *what* I'll do with my time now. I'll have to rethink life—get a new program for living—find some other interest."

"But what, you bozo?" he hissed.

"Well, I don't know," I mumbled. "Travel. Cooking. Theater. Fitness."

"You sound like the feature pages of a newspaper. You sound like the department headings in a news magazine."

"Religion. Books. I'll read again—I haven't had time in years. Tricking takes so much time. You think about it when you're not doing it, and when you're doing it, you're wondering if he really likes you. I know it won't be easy. I've tried to stop tricking before—it was like trying to leave a discotheque. You say you'll wait for a good song to leave on and end up sitting through some lousy ones. And then, when the good song *does* come, it makes you want to stay for some more. It's hard, saying that was my last trick."

My friend sighed, expelling a stream of smoke, and looked irritated at me, then the wall, then me again. "You can't stop tricking. Tricking is life. Tricking is the only adventure we can take that does not require a yacht, a Lear jet, and a Mediterranean island. It is life itself. And it is what we were made to do."

"I used to agree with you," I said. "When you first come out, it's how you learn everything about yourself and the world. It's the way you find your first lover, or at least how much rent someone is paying for a comparable apartment. But then you grow older, and as you become more of a person, with tastes, wisdom, appreciation, beliefs, you become less of a Trick. You go out and you think, *There's more to me than my sexual quotient. I'm a man. With a rich accumulation of detail. I can't reduce myself to a trick.* And you think it's a terrible prison, a language with only one word, that we are forced to speak because we have no other. And it seems the most stupid, reductive, and sterile exchange between people there could possibly be. You lose heart. You finally say, *This is getting you nowhere,* give the man your toaster, and say, 'You're my last trick.' "

But my friend had not really been listening—he had used the time to mull over in his mind the problem presented. "Perhaps the truth is you've been tricking badly. You've been simply inept. Choosing the wrong tricks."

"Evidently!"

"You've tricked the way women go through bathing suits in a bin in a bargain basement. As if all you can do is try the one within reach at the moment. Tricking cannot be done that way. You have to be smart. You must pick and choose."

"Buy why? Since anyone can turn into a lover," I said.

"Nonsense!" he said. "That only shows you've had no idea what you were doing. You should know three things in tricking," he said, holding up three fingers. "What you want, what you offer, how far you can trade up. Everyone wants to trade up in tricking."

"I don't want to trade up," I said. "I just want *him.*"

"Describe," he said.

"A lean, quiet man with glasses who's bright. And calm. And has a good sense of humor. And loves *me.*"

"Oh forget it," he said in a dark voice.

"Why?"

"It's too specific," he said. "It doesn't exist. Or if it does, it's married. The good ones are all married. They snap them right up."

"But why don't *I* snap them up? That's the problem—why don't my tricks want to marry me?"

He stared at me. "Would *you* marry you?" he said. There was a reverberating silence. The cat yawned—once, twice. A horn honked in the street below. "*That* is the question. The question everyone *has* to ask himself, and no one dares."

"Well," I said. "I think so. I hope so. Would *you* marry me?"

"Don't be silly," he said. "I'm your friend."

"And there is the problem," I said. "Friends get affection, tricks get good-bye."

"No one said it wasn't screwed up," he said. Then he sat gloomily smoking for a while, and finally he extinguished his cigarette, held his hands palm-up to the sky, and said with a shrug, "Maybe that *was* your last trick. Let's go to lunch, then Canal Jeans."

But of course it wasn't—though I left the black T-shirt glowering like a B-movie actress in the corner of the bar, my period came later that summer, and I went out desperate for human contact. To stop tricking is to stop life, in some terrible way. You feel guilty when you let a trick go. *What's wrong with me?* you ask yourself. *Getting old?* That was perhaps part of it. Sometimes tricking seems juvenile. Glowering in the corner of the bar that night, the black T-shirt looked like a junior high school I once went to, and which I walked past years later and paused beside to watch, through the wire fence, the kids playing games with each other on the field. It is easy to be funny about tricking and dangerous to be serious about it. But sometimes you're pooped. I told myself I had a bad cold coming on the evening I left the black T-shirt unpicked up in the bar, but it was almost a month or more before the menstrual cycle hit me again, and I went out looking for—what other option do we have?—a new and inspiring person I'd never met before.

This time *I* was black T-shirt, but not so desperate and gloomy—I was calm, nerveless, afloat on the incoming tide of desire, watching the Olympics in a bar. Love crystallized on a man nearly as indifferent to me as I'd been to black T-shirt. I followed him out into the parking lot, and he kindly asked me home. He was tall, rangy, lean, wearing glasses, intelligent, calm, and getting over the lover of two years he'd divorced only six months before. The sex left me with the conviction he'd do nicely for the rest of my life. When it was over he said, "I have to get up at five tomorrow." I took my cue. Last names were not exchanged. He put on a brown robe and gave me directions out of the city. Saying good-bye we hugged. When we went out onto the porch, he noticed two thick envelopes at our feet and bent down to pick them up. "They're from my ex," he said. "He must have dropped them here while we were inside, because they weren't here when we came in."

These envelopes were so plump I could not think them love letters—they had to be contracts, or applications to a university. My heart went out to the man who had dropped them off (was he watching us now from behind a hedge up the street?), because we were both now in love with the same man: the still center of the storm turning the envelopes over in his beautiful hands. What discipline I showed descending the stairs and entering my car! Whatever a Trick is, he knows what is expected of him. No toaster from this man—there would be others besides me. The night was cool and fragrant. The directions he gave led me flawlessly out of the city's knot of expressways into the dark countryside—an extension, somehow, of his masculinity. As I drove home I wondered what the future held. Sometimes a trick puts you out of commission for a while—the memory so good, you wish to honor it, the encounter so fine there is little chance the next one will be anything but depressing in comparison. Or he may send you out again for the same reason a man with a hangover reaches for a drink the next day. You don't know you're a trickster till long after you've become one—like the man who realizes he is an alcoholic only when he finds himself facedown in the bathroom at eight in the morning when he is supposed to be dressing for work. "Do you consider yourself promiscuous?" someone asks one day, and you don't know quite what to say.

When I got home the next day, I called my friend up and said, "Listen. I want you to help me fill out a form. I want to apply for a Guggenheim—I want a grant."

"For what?"

"I want about two thousand dollars," I said, "to answer an entire page of model and masseur ads in the *Native*."

"Now you're talking," he said. "Come on over, and I'll help you with the essay."

The Last Train From Cold Spring, N.Y.

M<small>ADAME</small> D<small>UPIN</small> C<small>LOSED</small> the great oaken doors of the institute behind her, turned, in the echoing entrance hall, and began speaking in the weary but polite voice of someone who has given this speech many times already. "Sex," she said, gently touching her thigh with the clipboard she carried, "is of course a profound stratagem of the psyche that we will never fully understand. The skin, as Dr. Villechaise has said, needs to be touched. And yet in one respect we may say it is no more complicated than a trip to Paris—*one does not go there to worry about bombs.* The contemporary individual must be able," she said, turning and leading us down a long white hall, "to say, after each erotic episode, what Piaf said about her entire life: *Je ne regrette rien.*" The clipboard slapped her thigh crisply this time. "To achieve this, we supply our client not merely with technique but, more importantly, the psychological foundation on which to build a preference for same."

"You mean," said one of the women in our group, "behavior modification."

"If you like," shrugged Madame Dupin. "But bear in mind," she said, "that some of our clients were, till recently, extremely active. I do not know how many of you are from the New York area, or familiar with the psychosis, if it is that, but even the best-intentioned sometimes fall by the wayside. Massage leads to a kiss, and a kiss leads to fellatio, and fellatio leads to what is now out of the question," she said, raising her clipboard to her waist and resting both hands upon it. Behind her stretched a long white corridor lined with doors, some open, some closed. "A brief walking tour of the classes in progress will give you some idea of our efforts to break this lethal chain," she said, and turning on her heel, she walked down the hall, stopped beside the doorway of the first classroom, and turned, allowing us to peer inside. "This is one of the introductory courses for incoming students in—*Elementary Frottage.*"

"The Princeton Rub," she said, for the benefit of one of the journalists scribbling all this down in a notebook.

We looked into the large room led by an instructor in a white smock, lecturing what looked like men of all ages dressed in white cotton shorts and sneakers, facing one another in pairs. "Frottage," said Madame, "which more people than you would imagine think is an event in horse shows, is one of the oldest of safe-sex activities and can be employed in a variety of circumstances, including the outdoors. In *Advanced Frottage*, the pupils are naked. For those who fear even frottage," she said, moving across the hall and nodding at the doorway of the opposite classroom in which a smaller group of men faced each other in pairs massaging their own nipples, "there is *No-Contact Frottage,* which is to say autoerotic frottage, in which the frottage occurs, like so much else these days, on a purely visual level. We have, of course, all cases," she said, slapping her clipboard against her thigh and moving forward down the long tiled corridor, "all levels of anxiety. Given the principle of the germ, as Dr. Villechaise has pointed out, there is no limit to which fear will not go! One has only to think of Howard Hughes. And, I must say, we see all types on the spectrum of fear and loathing. Some come because they find themselves incapable of safe-sex restraint, others merely to strengthen their defenses. We have classes that familiarize the student with spermicides, prophylactic gels, condoms, and a variety of household bleaches. Here, in the main salon," she said, pausing at two large doors open to an enormous hall still decorated with moose heads and windows of stained glass, "*Intercrural Copulation. Faux* sodomy. Between the legs. Perfect, one of our earlier visitors said, for an age of *faux marbre.*" She gave a wintry smile.

"In the next room," she said, resuming her official voice, moving down the hall, "*Introduction to Massage.* In the room opposite," she continued, turning in her high heels on the polished floor to indicate with a minimal gesture of her clipboard the classroom on the right, "*History and Eroticization of Condoms.* Next, *Mutual Masturbation.*" She walked forward, and stopped, allowing us to view a room full of men tugging at their gonads. "This course includes special seminars for those embarrassed about the size of their penis," she said, "and those who cannot stop feeling that they are only nine years old when they do this with another man. There are vast, vast terrains, enormous psychological blocks we must overcome," she said, resuming her tour and reaching out to snip off a dead leaf on a potted ficus tree. "Not everyone can accept safe sex, as you well know," she said. "Some say it is simply not sex! For them we have—discussion groups."

She leaned forward to open the large mahogany door of yet another salon containing a long table surrounded by students, one of whom insisted with a distraught expression on his face, "For me sex is surrender, merging, giving oneself up! For me, sex is—Love!" His classmates began to hiss loudly.

"It takes time," Madame said in a low voice, as she quietly closed the door and moved on down the hall. "What many do not realize is that the age of promiscuous, anonymous sex was also a *sentimental, romantic* age! The real romantics are, of course, our most difficult challenge. To them, sex that is rational, circumscribed, premeditated is not *sincere.* Sex to them must be a surrender, a loss of self—as you just heard Curtis say. They are searching, through physical love, for what Saint Theresa experienced through mystical trances. We lock their doors at night," she said, looking over her shoulder. "And prohibit their participation in the group activities the naturally celibate, restrained, rational are allowed, such as bridge, movies, dance." She leaned forward and opened another door; we saw a large white room, empty but for one man in the corner, seated on a stool, facing the wall. "Edgar," said Madame Dupin in her cool, quiet, perfectly modulated voice, "the so-called Sex Pig of Gramercy Park. A man who all his life has been incapable of sleeping with anyone who was *not* a stranger, in circumstances that were anything *but* dark and filthy, with accoutrements—like bottles of butyl nitrite, cans of Crisco—that were anything *but* safe. Placed in the sensory deprivation tank, even there he caused trouble, ejaculating into the water and stopping up the filtering system. For a week we were without hot water. It takes time," she said and closed the door.

A young man came toward us down the hall, accompanied by a security guard in a blue uniform. "Bruce," said Madame Dupin in a low voice, nodding at the student walking past us with a subdued, smoldering expression, "has never quite gotten over his days in the men's rooms of the IRT stations. Last night he jumped one of the new arrivals in the lavatory. This afternoon we will exhaust him with calisthenics. Running, swimming, rope climbs can reduce even the randiest man to a whimpering wreck who craves but one thing—sleep. By seven o'clock, Bruce can —if we have done our work well—barely pick up a fork."

She moved the clipboard to her side. "His mental problem is harder to deal with. After all, he is trapped. He says safe sex is not sex. But he does not wish to die. Ergo, he cannot have unsafe sex. If you want sex, it must be safe. If it is not sex, then why do it? Because it is the only sex possible. And so we go with them, round and round, like rats on a treadmill. It is not good," she said, "being a romantic homosexual these days. Unless, perhaps, one is—how do you say?—a daughter of Bilitis."

She stopped before the open door of a small auditorium, empty except for two men on stage, one dressed in a khaki raincoat, the other in leather chaps, jacket, and cap. "We have many students gifted in the arts," said Madame in a low voice, "and we of course welcome all therapeutic avenues. Recently, one of our juniors proposed the idea of allegory—as used in the medieval morality play—as a means for acting out some of the more common anxieties. In this play, the man in the raincoat plays the penis. The man in leather is the homosexual who refuses to have sex with a rubber. Primitive, perhaps, but useful for those impervious to other approaches, or even the illiterate, in minority neighborhoods. _Ecoutez._"

Our little group—composed of parents, relatives, friends of present or prospective students, members of the press, and people who had come up the Hudson to see Boscobel (in our case) and stumbled up the wrong driveway—turned their faces to the stage. "Isn't a man in a raincoat better than no man at all?" the actor was saying. "Isn't the thought of what lies beneath the raincoat enough? Didn't you like me when we spoke in the bar?"

"G'wan," said the other actor, "get outta here."

"This play has the audience in tears," whispered Madame as she led us down the hall.

"Jason," she said, stopping before the doorway of what was evidently an art studio and nodding at a young man

making charcoal drawings of spouting penises on an easel,
is sublimating his sexual anger by drawing what he misses.
Interestingly enough, a tremendous nostalgia for orgasm
is seen in almost all his work," mused Madame Dupin,
resuming her walk down the long white corridor. "That
mysterious validation, the goal, one might say, of the sexual
frenzy—the production of *seed*."

"Do they know why this is so?" said a member of our
group.

"Several hypotheses have been advanced," said Madame
in her clear, cool voice. "The belief that this proves one
has pleased one's partner. The desire to validate one's own
performance. Or something more hormonal, perhaps: the
blind desire of the sperm cell to see light, to fertilize the
egg. Even when there is, of course, no egg in sight—for
miles! It is the estrangement from the production and
ingestion of semen that has produced a withering effect,
one might say, in so many homosexual men. Consider the
Sex Pig who, after using a rubber, still demands that his
partner ingest the contents of same. The desire for fatal
fluid is one of our most fundamental roadblocks. Fortu-
nately, now that semen is as threatening to human life as,
say, plutonium, something similar to the Geiger counter
has recently been developed in Switzerland, and we are
able to detect even minute particles by merely inserting
the device into the rectum of suspected students."

"What happens then?" asked Ramon.

"An alarm goes off in my office," replied Madame. "Of
course, one cannot get very far from here if you do run
away. Sing Sing is only a few miles downriver. Last week
we caught one of our sophomores selling cockrings after
Lights Out."

"And why is that forbidden?" asked another of our group.

"Because cockrings are part of the trappings of the past,"

said Madame as we continued down the hall, with only her voice and the sound of her high heels on the polished floor breaking the silence of this stone mansion above the Hudson, "when everyone lived purely for sensation. The cockring is alleged to increase the sense of the orgasmic moment."

"But my girlfriend wears one as a bracelet," said a woman in a zebra-print dress.

Madame shrugged. "Do not blame us for the desperation of the fashion industry. We live in an age of epidemic fads. *And* epidemics. But now I would like to show you our class in *Detachment* for that most difficult group—the romantics." She turned to us. "It is easy to be celibate for one month, two months, even three. But inevitably, this abstinence produces neurosis and *catastrophe*." She led us into a large gymnasium in which two dozen men hung in canvas jackets suspended on wires from the ceiling, twirling slowly. "This calms the romantics down," explained Madame, "and gives them a sense of distance from the sensual self, which is essential in those who will have to practice safe sex. These men," she said, looking up at the dangling figures, "were unable to change their habits and knew it. And what habits! The men you see above you would spend eight hours at the baths, have four or five partners, all of whom gave them pleasure, and then on the way home, riding the subway, find themselves next to another man they liked, invite him home, and have more sex. In other words, once was not enough. Ten times was not enough! Sex simply left them starving for more when they awoke the next day. Imagine such an existence," she sighed, her voice thinning as she leaned her head back to look up at them with the rest of us. "Imagine the turmoil, the conflict, the expenditure of energy, the draining of energy from other more useful activities. And imagine the *angst* once this central activity was aborted. Like taking Communion from the

Catholics! Like telling the knights there would be no more Crusades! You see them here, gaining a physical sense of that most difficult, but essential thing—renunciation!

"And now," she told us, lowering her gaze to earth and walking out of the room, "there are refreshments in the common room, where I will be glad to answer any questions you may have." We filed out silently after her.

She led us down the hall to a large living room whose high, mullioned windows offered a dramatic view of the Hudson River winding its way between forested bluffs. Like so many boarding schools and monasteries in the vicinity, this great Gothic estate—only five minutes' walk from the station in Cold Spring—had once been a plutocrat's dream; in this case, that of a German-American millionaire brewer. From its lordly perch above the Hudson, one could see the afternoon sunlight glinting on the river, and the clusters of sullen teenagers we'd had to walk through after descending from the train, lingering in the drab town park in their seedy jackets, smoking cigarettes, riding dirt bikes, waiting, as in some Stephen King novel, for It to appear.

Inside the Institute, however, an austere elegance prevailed. A large carved mahogany table was set with trays of cookies and petit fours, and glasses of sherry, one of which Madame Dupin picked up and raised in the direction of the two men who had been scribbling notes since the tour began. "May I, before we begin, offer a toast? To the press," said Madame Dupin, "who, in their way, have been the most important element of all in our campaign to spread the word about the need for safe sex. Because of you, gentlemen, millions of homosexual men live today in good health. And terror. *Prost!*" she said. She put her head back and drank the drink at once. Several of the guests followed suit, but, unlike Madame Dupin, began to sputter, spit, and cough violently upon finishing.

"What is this?" one woman gasped.

"An emetic that wipes out everything from the upper and lower colon," Madame calmly explained. "We are trying to develop a flavor that would allow us to offer it as a popular soft drink. This one is perhaps a bit off the mark. Please sit," she said, doing so herself. "One of the main problems we face," she continued as the group settled itself around the long table, "is rectal nostalgia—the feeling, in the middle of the afternoon, when the homosexual least expects it, that he would prefer to be sitting *on* something. This, of course, is precisely what we cannot allow, and so we have chosen to attack the problem at its root, so to speak—Dr. Sanchez, from Guayaquil," she nodded at a handsome man with a black mustache and glasses who stood talking with a colleague, both in white coats, at the end of the gallery, "is a pioneer in this technique. Cauterization of the nerve endings, we feel, is one of the best long-term solutions to the problem we face in this area."

("But how can you cauterize the heart," muttered Ramon under his breath to me.)

Another man said, "You mean the rectal equivalent of a lobotomy. The anal equivalent of—castration."

"Exactly," said Madame Dupin. "Though these words tend perhaps to sensationalize," she added in a gracious tone, nodding at a woman across the table, who then said, "Madame Dupin, what do you say to critics who claim that in actual fact only a small percentage of the population worldwide is infected and that really this fear is unnecessary for many who could be having perfectly normal sex lives at this time?"

"*Merde,*" said Madame.

"I beg pardon?"

"*Merde!*" said Madame. "I am well aware of this criticism, but I would ask you to consider the facts. The facts are these: There are three kinds of people—the man who is infected but does not know it, the man who is infected and knows it, and the man who is not infected. All three look exactly alike. Therefore, there is no way of knowing for sure. Tattoos have been suggested, but given the unfortunate historical precedent, and the popular distaste for same, this will never be a practical alternative. No, something else is required," she said. "Something on a more massive scale, something that is still but a premonition." Her voice took on a bardic quality, her head went back, her tongue flickered over her lips, as if in a trance; and then, just as suddenly, she caught herself and leaned forward. She rose, smoothed her skirt, and said, "I believe most of you are taking the seven forty-three back to Grand Central, and therefore I will bring to a close our little tour by walking you to the entrance. Max will take those of you who would like to ride in the minivan to the station, or, if you prefer, the walk is lovely, and only five minutes on foot. Thank you so much for coming. Further questions may be answered by our brochures."

She walked into the hall, turned and waited for us to catch up, and then, her high heels clicking again, we followed her down the long polished hall like so many ducklings. It was getting dark. The sun was setting behind the bluffs across the river and plunging the wooded cliffs, the river itself, into darkness. A crisp, exhilarating chill was in the air when Max opened the great wooden doors for us; outside, the van sat in the drive, motor running, its fenders covered with fallen leaves. From the big barn across the lawn we could hear the clatter of tap shoes.

Ramon turned to our hostess as the others entered the van. "Madame Dupin, you spoke of something else that is required, something on a more massive scale, to—solve this problem. May I ask what you had in mind?"

"Of course," she replied with a slightly warmer smile this time. "It has to do with something I was unable to discuss at length earlier in our talk—the internalization of safe-sex precepts, the eventual obsolescence of places like this institute. How, you ask? Very simple." Her eyes glowed, her voice became more animated as she stood in the Gothic foyer while the van drove off, and the shadow of the beer millionaire who had built this great Gothic pile—of his statue, that is—fell upon the three of us. "I predict that as the disease continues to spread and the news of it is transmitted widely, something very radical will happen to the way we regard the penis itself. *Comprends-tu?* The penis will no longer be what it has been till now—the Fountain of Life, the Nile overflowing its banks, the last wild, vital alternative to a sterile, mass-marketed, technological culture." She took Ramon by the arm and squeezed him with a grip so powerful his face went white. "The penis will become, I predict, an image of death—a dagger, a gun, a terrorist's bomb. The final stage of safe sex—its *ultimate* form—will be the transformation of the way we regard the penis itself, until external discipline and safe-sex techniques become altogether unnecessary, because— well, because—"

"What?" asked Ramon, as she ushered us out of the cold entrance hall onto the steps and placed herself behind the door, ready to close it for the night.

"The thought of sex with another man will be simply— nauseating!" said Madame Dupin. With that she smiled and closed the door with a solid, leaden click.

Ramon turned to me, pale in the wintry darkness, and said, "Almost but not quite! I have a date with John in the city at midnight. And the nine-thirty is the last train. Let's go!" And we both began running down the drive, eager to leave behind the muffled screams the clatter of tap shoes could not quite drown out. Just when we reached the gate, in fact, a red shoe landed in front of us—thrown from a window or hedge; in it was a stone, around the stone a piece of paper, which, unfolded, read: HELP ME GET OUT OF HERE BEFORE I DO SOMETHING DESPERATE I'M SO HORNY I'M ABOUT TO EXPLODE But we could not—we broke into a run; just as the Institute collapsed behind us in a terrible roar, and the noise of Ramon, yelling to wake me from my dream.

Good Sex/Bad Sex

MOST PEOPLE HAVE A list, I was thinking one night this winter after everyone had gone to bed. Mine are: a man in San Francisco who was a bartender; an Italian-American ballroom dancer; a man who ran a guesthouse in upstate New York; a French photographer who had what the trash novels call "silken skin"; a houseboy in Miami; a man in Jacksonville who had dozens of framed photos of his family on the shelf, et cetera. It wasn't merely their bodies. It wasn't even that *they* were good sex (though some of them were)—it was the circumstances of the encounter, my own condition at the time: the empty house on Fire Island the night the lease was up; the excitement of a person, a season, a place. Yet I still search for some common trait. Early in my homosexual life, I asked a friend what he thought good sex was. "It's when," he said, "the other person wants you as much as you want them." That's pretty astute and yet, like all definitions of this subject, it doesn't cover all of the above; the man in Jacksonville had a sick stomach and apologized for just lying there, but whereas in the old days I considered this the essence of bad sex—selfish and passive—his inertia suited me fine; that was the mood I was in years later that night.

His apology made it all right—in recognizing the fact that sex is something two people contribute to. He was concerned about his contribution. We all are. "People who are bad sex will go through their whole lives never knowing it," a friend once said, "because no one ever tells them." This may be true—bad sex, like bad breath, is a topic taboo—but most people want to do well. We all get our grades fairly early, in fact; sex is in a sense an exam one takes over and over again. We all want an A. We were brought up to get A's, and to be popular. Our first desire is simple: Everyone should want to sleep with us. (And us alone, as Auden said.) Everyone doesn't, as it turns out. Only some. So we go to the gym, cut our hair, trim our stomachs, use bottled water. And we still can't quite believe that, after *us*, other people don't just pack their bags and go home from the baths completely satisfied. We aim to please. Aren't we Hot Men? Hot Men, we assume, have incredible sex *every time*. Why? The experts differ; some say it is physical (a magic cock) and some say it is all in the mind. But in the high school of sex homosexuals are trapped in—clutching our damp, well-thumbed report cards—heads turn as Johnny goes by between classes (or tricks) and people whisper, "Professor Fainstock gave him a ninety-eight." Or (in real life): "In*cred*ible sex."

Perhaps Johnny is not the same for everyone out in the halls—we could ask homosexuals across America to submit their Top Ten to a central computer, of course, and see if the same names appear, and award them Tonys next spring—but we can all probably name a few people who were good for *us*. For if bad sex leaves you ashamed, fills you with regret, makes you want to hide from the person with whom you've shared this debacle, good sex makes you want to give honor where honor is due. Good sex imbues the person who provided it with a permanent halo. The sight of him brings a smile to your lips, and even though you are one of those people who prides himself on never revealing what someone you slept with does in bed (much less the dimensions of Mr. Happy), you murmur despite yourself as he walks by, "*Such* good sex." He made you content. The memory remains, or something more complicated. (Robert Myers said it best: "Bad sex leaves you depressed. Good sex leaves you suicidal.") And you both honor and envy the person, because you assume he brings this pleasure to everyone lucky enough to share his mattress, or house, or blue jeans. Why? It is his talent, his genius. He has a gift. He's on a wavelength as real as that emitted by a radio station. He has a certain animal magnetism (which Scott Fitzgerald—assessing himself with the ruthless objectivity he brought to romantic matters—felt superseded beauty in the realm of sex); or a certain intelligence "intelligent" people often lack. For it is fairly obvious the man who knows music, literature, business, or physics may be what one friend of mine called a "sexual fumbler." Some people are connoisseurs, always pick the right partner, or inspire the one they are with; and others are simply myopic.

And we want to be the former, of course; we are always concerned with our report card. It is both good in itself and a kind of power. To be good sex is to have a hold on other people. Sex is a way of binding others to us. It makes the phone ring. We want to shout like Mayor Koch, "How'm I doing?" And each time someone we sleep with—whether we love him or not—does not want to have sex with us again, we feel in some strange way we have *flunked*. We failed to cast a spell, to enchant, to enthrall; all of us want deep down to detain other men in their flight—to be Circe and have a garden of studs around us with rings in their noses, rooting among our organic vegetables. We want not only sex whenever we want it, and with whom we want, but endlessly, like those civilized older men we met when we came to the city who had a circle of six or seven they invited over to listen to music and to have (it was assumed) incredible sex.

For the dream of good sex persists even though so much of it for most people is brief and mundane and disappointing. A friend once said to me, "Sex you can get anywhere," in a tone that implied, *Therefore it is not worth very much.* To me the fact (in New York, at least) was a program for living, for years. When young I was in love, in a way, with sex itself. It astonished me on certain days, walking down Third Avenue at three in the afternoon, that each man I passed had a penis. When the T-shirt that says SO MANY MEN, SO LITTLE TIME first appeared, the laugh it induced was profound—that was it, unfortunately, exactly. (Or as a friend in San Francisco redefined it, SO MANY MEN, SO LITTLE NERVE.) But inevitably the primal bliss of embracing men—this dream you thought could never come true—gives way to distinctions. Each time you sleep with someone is different. Some are awful. Some are great. I thought it possible to find good sex in particular places, at particular times. For instance, sex was better in San Francisco. ("In San Francisco you have sex," said a friend. "In New York you wait for people to come.") Waiting for people to come never happened in San Francisco—either because we were on vacation there (the subjective theory) or because the homosexuals who lived in that city had gone there to *be* homosexual, had fewer distractions, and were more devoted to its central ritual (the objective theory). Living in New York, I had to devise some sort of logarithmic tables of sex based on such questions as: Were the baths best on Friday, Sunday, or Tuesday nights? Did rain make people go out or stay in? Did a full moon induce craziness? Did fall make me horny? Because once, while waiting in front of my apartment for the rain to stop, I met someone, went home with him, and had good sex, I stood in front of my apartment for years afterward when it rained, as if by repeating the circumstances I could reproduce the sex. Rain, sleet, snow, weekends, week nights, fashionable/unfashionable baths, bars, depression, elation, five-thirty, or after midnight—I really thought, like a duck hunter observing the clouds, that there was a certain constellation of conditions that produced good sex. Then one sunny Monday I was walking home at five o'clock when a friend came out of the baths, and I said, "How was it?" for this was a time I had never investigated. He could have gone down the usual list—the people were hot/not hot, the atmosphere wild/boring—but he merely waved his hand and called, across the hood of a taxi, a line that summed up my thinking at the time: "If you're in the mood, *they're* in the mood!"

So simple! Yet I went out often when I was not in the mood. It was a habit, routine, a way of life, the well-known mistake: of using sex for everything but a dandruff shampoo. Most sex was average, as most days are average, but one couldn't accept that. And I wavered between thinking the reason was physical—the penis, over and out—or spiritual: an affinity sometimes present between two people searching for what they don't often know. Once a friend pointed out a man on the dock at Fire Island and said, "He's incredible sex. All drug addicts are. The skin is so sensitive." But was sex confined to the skin? Or the mind? Very few people, I finally concluded, really understood what sex can be; but I didn't know if this was because (a) they were clods; or (b) I did not release the god in them. For in all good sex—whatever its cause, I decided—the god was present. During good sex one was inspired—not merely by the person you had sex with but by all those currents that mysteriously fed your mood at that moment: happiness, depression, or the sheer erotic energy that builds up in us from time to time like static in a carpet, or some menstrual movement. There are days in New York when you are so filled with cumulative lust you feel yourself divine; no trick could possibly be worth your adoration;

until, you realize, anyone will do. Most of the time, however, you go out to find sex without the god; because you
are bored, or lonely, or have wasted the day, and stand in
the park or hallway of the baths rubbing your body against
another like two children rubbing sticks at a campfire to
see if a spark will ignite. You operate in a numb state of
what is really despair. And you wonder, in the words of
Lana Turner, Where Love Has Gone.

In college I remember my roommate, on the phone one
day with an older friend just engaged, turning to us and
saying after he'd hung up, "Kyle says the best sex is with
someone you love." How few of us ever find out. When
you first fall for people, the mixture of love and lust, sentiment and sex, are pretty even. They soon are sundered.
At first their separation—the realization that tricking is
done with no strings attached—horrifies the idealistic
homosexual who wants to re-create the sort of marriage
he's seen in his family. Then, after years of reality, he
comes to separate the two himself, and sex becomes an
encounter, like playing handball or wrestling: an athletic
engagement of two men—and he asks himself: *Am I, or
the world, growing more pornographic?* No doubt pornsex ex-
isted before pornography, but it is tempting to think of it
as something people would not pursue—as La Rochefou-
cauld said of falling in love—had they not read about it
first. Pornsex sets up new insecurities, of course. People
already busy comparing themselves with the men they
meet—the pecking order based on peckers—now had to
compare themselves with Al Parker. (We want the people
we sleep with to be on our level, somehow.) Pornsex can
be just what one needs—desperately—and is as elusive as
good sex of any sort, but as the staple of clonelife it becomes
reductive after a while. The heart still dreams of that miraculous marriage with another person you don't have to
perform for. Love means: no auditions. When the man in

middle age no longer finds pornsex even sexy, he begins to think that sex and sentiment should never have been sundered at all, like the friend from California who once wrote me on a postcard, "Thank God I never confused tricking with sex."

Most of us do, of course, and in that long career of good sex/bad sex, there have been acts one is ashamed of afterward; things one never forgets—which involve hurting someone's feelings or, occasionally, body. The first occur because in the end sex is—though we try to make it the opposite—irretrievably personal; the second because we do not all operate within the code of ethics we should. Feelings, pride, self-esteem, deep desires, are always involved in sex. In all sex we are offering ourselves on some level for marriage. Sex is the one moment when the body and spirit are the same item. And it treats us, curiously, the way we treat it. H. told me in Paris he did not like people to think about sex or make it complicated. But though I shut up, I thought, *I cannot fail to notice what he seems to want and try to understand.* (Though another person advised me years ago as the road to good sex, "Just think of the penis. Blot out everything else.") Good sex may be, after all, as mythic as El Dorado. (The few times I had all I wanted, day and night, I felt—to my astonishment— bored and impatient; hoping, as the sacred event occurred repeatedly, the phone would ring.) Good sex may be a dream we look back on, or forward to, but rarely know in the present. Often I've waited for the person to leave so I could recollect our sex—like Wordsworth and the daffodils—without the insecurity and politics of the actual encounter. Curious ideal! In one's youth, sex is rarely examined intellectually—one is too absorbed in learning it. Too deeply under its spell. In middle age—after the spell is broken—it becomes something else; especially sex between people of the same gender. Sex between people of the same gender is—strictly speaking—absurd. Nothing can come of it, from a dynastic point of view. It does not produce life. It's divorced from function—and hence, pure form. (I watched over the years this form evolve. "I had sex last night," said the dazed friend I met one morning stepping off his lover's boat onto the boardwalk in the Pines, "with his *elbow*.") Homosexuality and heterosexuality answer the same instincts but differ in the sense that the former never evolves into the sublimated eros of family bonds. It remains sex—and we remain its prisoners, who find it hard to remember that sex was once life, not death. But it was. One hot summer day in Central Park, I met a man from Boston who had a room at the Y, ran back to a friend's apartment to get a popper, grabbed a beer, and raced back through the park. It was ninety degrees, the sound of drums being played at Bethesda Fountain came through the trees, the beer can was cold to my touch, the sweat ran down my face, the leaves of the trees were all coated with dust, as I ran to the Y thinking, *This is what it means to be alive!* Such moments are gone now, but in mulling over good and bad sex, it is interesting I think that I hardly remember the sex itself (it was brief, pornographic, not bad) with the blond Bostonian; what I recall so vividly are the drums, sweat, dust on the leaves, cold can of beer, popper bouncing in my pocket, as I ran *to* what I was sure would be good sex on that hot August day. What I remember is the feeling of being alive.

Tuesday Nights

TUESDAY NIGHTS WE meet in a Quaker meetinghouse on a quiet residential street in Gainesville —a city in north-central Florida—just two blocks from the campus of the university. The discussion group is several years old now. "It started out at The Drugstore," says a friend who has gone to it intermittently since the beginning, "and it was *won*derful. Kids would come in and say, 'I think I'm gay, but I'm not sure.' People would *weep*. It was so moving, and wide open. But then everything was in those days," this nostalgic hippie sighs. "Then it was taken over by an assistant professor who used it as a *trick farm* [the sixties becoming the seventies] until one night he found himself speaking to an empty room [the seventies becoming the eighties]. He had slept with everyone, you see. So it lay fallow for a while, and now it's in its third phase. More sober and level-headed, but without those *won*derful moments of revelation." Indeed there is something middle-aged about the group, perhaps, run by a doctor who, amazingly, comes up each week with a new speaker, topic, or film. The core group of faithful attendants comprises a psychiatrist, a schoolteacher, a writer, a librarian, a retailer, an attorney, and only occasionally— in the fall, when students come back to school—the freshmen who spill their souls (as in the old days) in a frenzy of coming out, and then never appear again. Where they go I do not know. The once-competing organization of gay and lesbian students at the university is now defunct; a charismatic leader, since graduated, has not been replaced by anyone, and a quarrel over funds with the student government has left its speaker's program in disarray.

There are always a few wild cards, too, on Tuesday nights, and that is part of the reason one goes: to see the person you've never seen before, or the ones who come every three months or so; the recently arrived student or assistant professor who know no one in town yet and bring with them a burst of northern energy from Ann Arbor or Berkeley, and then vanish again. But mainly one finds The Group —of ten or twelve men who come every week, and even dine together in a different restaurant each Thursday, and who constitute what a golf foursome or poker club must have for my father: a dependable bunch of men with whom one can relax, unwind, and talk on a weekly basis. For what I prize most about this evening, perhaps, as I sit beside a whirring fan in summer, or a space heater on cold nights, is what characterizes this particularly leafy street, this plain wooden house: a certain camaraderie and calm.

The house is shared—someone said—by a fugitive family from Central America, but I have no way of knowing if this is so, since we are the only ones in it on Tuesday nights. But this rumor emphasizes the marginal, sub-rosa nature of our shared identity . . . even within the homosexual population itself. There must be three to five thousand gay men in Gainesville, but here at the meeting there are only twenty or so. I have friends in this town who wouldn't be caught dead here on Tuesday nights. Ten years ago I would never have come to a meeting of this sort. People who belonged to groups like this, or went to the gay churches, were, I assumed, people who did not have the nerve to look for a partner in the actual world: the baths, beaches, and bars. In the old days tricking was the way we met people. But things are reversed now. The idea of tricking seems absurd. The mating dance has slowed down considerably. Everyone here hopes he will meet someone, I suppose—though most of them are attached already; perhaps only when the problem of sex has been solved does one have time or energy to spare for its sublimations. But that does not explain Gaytalk entirely. To meet somebody may be the reason I went to my first meeting—a reason reflected in the behavior of lesbians who come once, find no other women, and do not return—because the bars in Gainesville are cliquish (friends talking to each other, while the hapless stranger swims around like a penguin among ice floes that are already occupied). But the second time I came—after giving up, and going back to the bars for a year—I was having an AIDS anxiety attack.

That night, by coincidence, a male nurse from Ocala was giving a talk on this subject, and having fears aired in this manner helped, the way calling the Gay Switchboard—though you use it only once or twice in your life—in a strange city helps. The third time I went back, it was a blend of these two motives: fear and longing. Fear and longing seem to cancel each other out these days. Fear and longing are, furthermore, played out differently in a town this size, which doesn't provide the vacuum of anonymity a city like New York does—a vacuum through which sparks fly so easily—because the man you go home with will almost surely be in the bar the next night. But fear and longing persist, and this place seems the perfect compromise. Here the plague seems a bit removed, as I listen to a lecture on Michelangelo on this plain wooden folding chair as the fan whirs and I watch a student come back to the boardinghouse next door, his blond head passing under the porch light. I feel, in fact, as if I'm in church.

From the first time I went, I have considered this a sort

of prayer meeting, in fact. The gathering together, the communion (of minds), the calm, the straw basket that is passed afterward to obtain donations, all remind me of church. No one stands up to confess deep dark secrets, or testifies, but there is, on our folding chairs, beside the fake pine-paneled walls, under a bulb in the ceiling, the atmosphere of an evening service in some country church. Here for an hour passion is transcended, if that is not too fancy a way of putting it. Here for a moment we enjoy what a friend in New York (who greets with joy an inclination to go to the movies instead of the baths) would call "a neutral activity." Here we do something that does not center around cruising. That, for gay men, is church. Gay men, of course, went to church as much as other children, but, when they grew up, found themselves outside the church and the culture they were otherwise part of. Hence Dignity, the gay synagogue, AA, psychiatrists, gay books, and Gaytalk on Tuesday nights. Times have changed, and changed radically, but each one of us is still trying to find the same old things: sex, and love, and self-respect.

Sex, love, and self-respect are hard enough to balance in life, period, without having to do it as a person whose biological identity seems at variance with his sexual one. How to integrate our homosexuality with the rest of our selves, our lives—our family, our society, our upbringing —was a problem a minority, not a majority, of the gay men I knew were able to solve before the plague. Most of us just kept everything in compartments. Most of us led double, triple, quadruple lives, changing costumes as actors do, masking our intelligence, emphasizing our bodies, feeling our fate depended on the shape of our mustache, the size of our dick. But you can juggle the apples of discord only so long. When desire begins to burn off, like morning haze, it leaves the rest of our personalities more visible. "I've read all of Proust and Henry James, I just got a promotion at the bank to systems manager," a friend wrote me in 1977. "So what am I doing at four A.M. in Sheridan Square, hailing a cab with shit on my dick?" *Having the time of your life,* I would have answered had we both been twenty-one. But we were not, and that was part of the problem: What youth and lust camouflage, age and abstinence bring into relief—the contradictions of being gay. The plague has only increased the vividness of the questions in those who've survived thus far. It has made dangerous the sex that was used to answer all doubts, cater to all moods, avoid all problems. "I belong to a GMHC Safe Sex Study Group," the friend who had his moment of truth at four A.M. in Sheridan Square in 1977 writes me this week. "Everyone is either a little or very crazy, and all ask the same question: If every gay man in the Rancid Apple is terrified of getting AIDS, why can't these dizzy clones settle down and play house with one another?"

It's one of the questions I think about as I sit in the Quaker meetinghouse, miles from the epicenter, but still part of the plague. ("The virus is here, in the community," says one of the doctors. Just recently, three men died of AIDS in Gainesville in one week.) When the plague began, I thought homosexual society would wither away—if men could not sleep with one another, why would they go out to baths, bars, or beaches? I was wrong. There is still some need to be together—even to hear someone deliver a book report on Kaplan's biography of Walt Whitman, or a history of the Mattachine Society. The topics vary in importance, no doubt, to each individual. A graduate student describes a study of early childhoods of people who later became homosexual. The next week a lawyer explains the mechanics of making wills in which a homosexual partner is the beneficiary. A psychiatrist surveys the APA's definition of homosexuality over the years. A man reviews local political candidates (pointing out that a public endorsement by our group may in fact harm, rather than help, the candidate we prefer). The pastor of the local gay church speaks, followed by a woman from a local department store who lectures on cosmetics. A teacher discusses the various charitable drives (Toys for Tots, Food for the Indigent on Thanksgiving) the group might participate in. A doctor brings in his favorite opera records. Another doctor, his favorite wines. In its improvised, eclectic course, the group moves forward like some snail, incorporating whatever enters its path, feeding on its members' expertise, which is more fun, I think, than something more strictly political. That would be too narrow. Homosexuality is more than politics; and more than sex; and under the ceiling bulb, while the students float by on bicycles outside on green summer evenings, this quiet room seems very much like Life. Moments of exquisite boredom (the classroom clichés of the visiting psychologist) are followed by breathless revelation—the student who lists his reasons for not telling his parents he's gay, and then tells us what his fraternity brothers said when he told them. These are the stories I love to hear. At the end of each meeting, we are asked to go around the room and introduce ourselves. Then the straw basket is passed from person to person, the speaker is thanked and applauded, and we stand up and talk to friends. When I first came here, I had none and fled to my car in a paroxysm of shyness—something newcomers still do—but now I linger with the rest on the sidewalk outside, like any congregation.

The modest, unstated proposition that Gaytalk rests upon is this: that the rational (Come, let us reason together) can bring into focus what is irrational (Eat my big dick, you worm). "Homosexuality," said Oscar Wilde, "is the problem for which there is no solution." But sitting here listening to men of different ages, circumstances, talk about their version of the problem, one feels that if there is

not—to the problem of Life, either—it is pleasing none-
theless to assume we can reach one. Hearing them argue
is an opportunity to stand back from the bewildering contradictions of being gay—to put things in perspective, to
talk, as reasonably as possible, about things that may not
be reasonable at all in real life. When we leave the Quaker
meetinghouse, I feel a magic circle has been broken. For
beyond the screen door is the real world, with its separate
compartments, its balancing act.

In fact most of us get in our cars after the discussion,
drive straight to the bar, and regroup inside its very different environment, talking to one another as our eyes
roam the room, checking out the patrons who did not come
to Gaytalk. (The modest, unstated proposition the bar rests
on is: Everything can still be solved with a lover). Would
Gaytalk be pointless without the Ambush afterward? Would
it be possible if once every six weeks I couldn't drive to
the Club Baths in Jacksonville—where men meet, but do
not discuss much? (There's a Gaytalk that takes place in
steamrooms.) I don't know. It's useless to pretend that sex
is *not* at the center of homosexual life—the reason these
men want to be with one another—and yet at this point
in time it (sex) seems less central than it used to be. Hence,
Gaytalk. The last slide of David—the ideal—fades from
the screen, and the speaker asks, "Are there any questions?" Lots, but no doubt they can't be answered. One
must still make the connection on one's own between Michelangelo and what waits outside, the minute one opens
that screen door—the screen door past which young men
ride on their bicycles, oblivious of the problems in which
they play the central role, immured in youth and beauty.

Trust

WE WERE SITTING on a porch in Florida this afternoon leafing through the portfolio of photographs a friend had brought over, half watching the butterflies in the geraniums, when I came to the portrait of a handsome man and asked who this was. A man in San Francisco, my friend replied, who had just walked out on his lover. "And you know what his exit line was?" he said. " 'When you get the night sweats, you'll know you've got it.' "

"What do you mean?" I said.

"He has AIDS," my friend said of the good-looking man with the mustache and wavy hair. "He had it when he began the relationship, but he told his lover if they kept a positive attitude, they wouldn't get it. Now, of course, the boyfriend's got it, and when it happened," he said, pointing to the photograph, "he packed his bags and walked out, saying, 'When you get the night sweats, you'll know you've got it.' "

"But—but—" I said, incredulous, dumbfounded, staring at this handsome man in the photograph, "who is he?"

"He's smart," said my friend. "He's a psychologist. He wanted to get AIDS."

"Wanted to?" I said.

"He went out to the baths, just when it began, when he knew it was dangerous, and put his ass up in the air," he said. "He wanted to get it."

"But how does the lover feel?" I said, pointing to the adjacent photograph, a man with a dark beard and friendly eyes. "The one he gave it to?"

"He has chronic hepatitis," my friend said. "His stomach is swelled out to here," he said, drawing a potbelly in the air. "He just thinks it's one more version of being dumped on by life."

When I first heard stories—like this one—I didn't believe them; they belonged to that realm of rumor in which the gossip is made up out of whole cloth, merely because it's so dramatic. No one would do that in real life, I thought. It just isn't believable. The first story I heard—about five years ago—involved the death of a decorator in New York whose brother flew east from California to attend the wake and stayed with a man I'll call Bob. The brother was attractive, and one evening after the wake, talking things over before the fireplace, Bob and the brother ended up having sex. When the sex was over, talking once more, Bob asked the brother what he would do with all the money he'd inherit from the decorator; the brother replied, "Spend it. I have AIDS, too."

Surely this was made up, I thought; no one could possibly do that. It's certainly true, as Scott Fitzgerald wrote, that a sense of the fundamental decencies is parceled out unequally at birth, but I could not even imagine the person who would knowingly expose another person to the virus. I had trouble with people who littered; I wanted them arrested and given the electric chair. I knew the junk that clogged the mangroves in which gay men cruised at Virginia Key in Miami, soiled the dunes at the gay beach south of Jacksonville, was proof that gay people, yes, *even gay people*, were slobs. But I had perhaps a rather exalted vision of homosexuals; I suspected, in some chamber of my heart, that they were, well, neater, nicer, more sensitive than the rest. Mayor Lindsay used to say, "The trouble

with New York is that there are too many slobs." But I
didn't include the gay community in that; I found it hard
to believe—and very discouraging—that they even littered.
But then a few years of the plague, and more stories of
this sort, passed, and the next one I heard about someone
I knew sounded a little more imaginable: A young man
just out of the hospital after a bout of pneumocystic pneumonia went to the Saint to celebrate, met someone, and
took him home. Hmmmm. One *would* go to the Saint to
celebrate, perhaps, that was not unlikely, and perhaps in
the mood created by the place, the dancing, one might
meet someone, and . . . but there it stopped. People do not
murder other people casually. Surely he would have told
the person he had just got out of the hospital, and so on.
    And then, shortly after hearing this story, I read about
Fabian Bridges. Fabian Bridges was just a newspaper article at first—about a male prostitute shunted back and
forth between two cities that didn't want him, because he
had AIDS and the judge thought the only solution was to
put him on a bus out of town. Put this way, I felt sorry for
Fabian Bridges; then I saw him in a documentary on television. On television Fabian Bridges was seen haunting
the seedier parts of cities (those blocks that look exactly
alike in Pittsburgh, Houston, Jacksonville, New York: the
dirty bookstores, the theaters, the parking lots), after being
asked by a doctor in the most patient, cajoling, restrained
manner, to stop having sex. Stop having sex was what
Fabian somehow seemed unable to do—though he voiced
a mild regret at having ejaculated inside a customer (a man
he'd come to like). This wistful regret was the only one
Fabian Bridges evinced; friends who saw the film explained him away with brain infection—the virus had already destroyed his ability to act morally. But I wasn't so
sure; it seemed possible to me Fabian Bridges was just one
of those horrors—a morally inert succubus drifting through

life without much will to do right or wrong. Who knows?
The gay community in Texas did what the courts and
police could not—took Fabian in, got him off the street—
and then death took him off the planet. But not before,
one assumes, he had taken others with him.

We read daily now of prostitutes of both sexes who refuse to stop working, even though they have AIDS. There
is an ex-American army sergeant being tried in Germany
right now for having had sex with three men and not telling
them he had the virus; the case has been clouded by the
fact that one of them, a Spaniard, also had AIDS at the
time. My, my. It just goes on and on. Admit the principle,
and there is no end to the permutations.

I was watching TV with a friend the evening the death
of Rock Hudson was announced. After asking me in a
curious voice why gay men were so promiscuous, my friend
then inquired, "Why did you *trust* one another?" The question gave me a moment's pause; I had never thought of it
in those terms before—terms of trust. I said, "Because
there was no reason not to. Everything could be cured with
some form of penicillin." Yet now that I reflect on it all,
it seems to me that not antibiotics but trust was the thing
that made that life possible: the assumption that the person
you slept with would not knowingly infect you with anything vile. Trust was the basis of the whole system—the
Visa card that sent you to Brazil, Berlin, or California with
the prospect of romance. (The thing that impelled people
to go there, soon after the plague appeared in New York,
in fact, on the assumption that It hadn't arrived in these
places yet.) There were exceptions to all this, of course. I
got crabs in those days more times than I could count; by
the twentieth time, I was less strict about waiting a few days
after dousing myself with A-200 before going out again.
I got amoebas and learned, after the fact, I'd been exposed
to hepatitis; but I considered most of these just occupa-

tional hazards, germs swimming in the community pool, and not the malicious, much less lethal, act of any particular person. True, there were nights when, at the baths, I would see a man leave someone's room and the door to that room open a moment later to take on a new visitor— and I would think, *The fat, lazy cow. Can't even go downstairs and shower between encounters.* And in my disgust I would eventually walk past that open door to see who the slob was. He was always someone ordinary, I mean, without any distinguishing marks that set him apart from everyone else at the baths; and that, of course, is the trouble with trust now.

The rumor that AIDS had been spread by an airline steward had been around several years; the version I heard featured an Australian on Air Qantas. The airline steward, of course, has always personified a certain aspect of gay life—the most complete version of the fantasy; to be a new face in Rome, Paris, Cairo, London, Madrid—all in the same week, to sleep not with everyone in your gym, but with the whole world. It seemed, at a certain age, the only thing to do; an adventure one would be a fool not to spend at least a year on. Promiscuity and jet travel were somehow twins—synergistic. How else to get It from a green monkey in the interior of Africa to a penthouse in New York? The tracing of Patient Zero in Randy Shilts's new book on AIDS is not only a dramatic case of mystery solving; it's the culmination of all those stories about this person—this gay person in whom I could not quite believe—that have been floating around for years now. No wonder the mainstream press picked up on it. It finally gives a face to what has been so far faceless. It crystallizes all the anger and moral outrage that have been gathering without an object. The steward from Air Canada reduces a force, a vast dilemma, to what even an age accustomed to institutional power hungers for—the story of a single human being making a choice between right and wrong, good and evil. Gaetan Dugas, apparently, made the wrong choice. Gaetan personifies, in what we've read of him so far, a recognizable type in gay life: the vain and careless Queen. The Pretty Boy with the not-so-pretty value system. The Moral Slob. The Femme, oh very, Fatale. Flying from place to place, the man at the baths who—I presume—opened his door a moment after the last man had left and did not bother to go downstairs to shower; who, when the lights came up, if what we read is true, commented casually on his Kaposi's sarcoma as "the new gay cancer. Perhaps you'll get it, too."

A friend with AIDS gave some advice about having sex nowadays that still seems excellent: "Have sex," he said, "as if everyone is infected." What better guide? Standing in the Jewel in New York, watching the men go up and down the aisle, I can easily imagine now that some have AIDS. (In fact, someone told me last week that people with AIDS go there.) Why not? What else would you do if you had AIDS? Would you not more than ever have to be there, to cruise, to forget, to feel alive? Fabian Bridges, Patient Zero, are only extreme versions of something in many of us; we have all fudged reality a bit in the past five years, I suspect—behaved with standards that now seem to us lax and self-deluded. Indeed, the longer the plague goes on, and the more pervasive our exposure to it, the more unappetizing sex becomes—sex that seems risky, that is. But this psychological barrier, this distaste, was not always there; it took years to coalesce and solidify. The trouble is we know now that a person can give someone AIDS in several moral states—not knowing he has it, knowing he has it but not thinking what he does is dangerous ("Just keep a positive attitude!"), knowing he has it and passing it on out of despair, revenge, indifference, hatred, selfishness, or sheer amorality; having a hole where the conscience should be, or a vengeful feeling that what the community gave to him, he can give back. It's the same principle, after all—the man who goes out with crabs and the man who goes out with AIDS. Only crabs can be killed with A-200; the virus cannot. And with that fact, all trust dissolves.

The truth is most people are not amoral, most of them care very much about not endangering someone they have sex with, but the fact that some are, is enough to shut down the whole system. It's a bit like the Tylenol scare—most of the bottles on the shelf were surely safe, but the possibility that one of them might contain poison was enough to make the manufacturer withdraw the product. AIDS destroys trust. We cannot possibly investigate, much less be responsible, for what the man we are attracted to has done with the past five or seven years of his life. We can't guarantee ourselves. This limits sex with each passing year. It shuts down a whole system of behavior, a community; it builds a wall between each of us. AIDS is a form of pollution; in this case, polluted semen and blood. We've spoiled even that. AIDS is a form of terrorism—sex becomes Paris the summer the bombs went off. Nobody goes. Like Central Park—empty at night because everyone's afraid of muggers—homosexual life becomes a vast empty space from which everyone has withdrawn. We look at one another not merely as appetizing possibilities, possible boyfriends, fantasies, pleasure—we look at each other as lethal instruments, threats, dangers, obstacle courses, things one would have to sift through a whole host of tests in order to eat. Sodomy—the central ritual from which all else proceeded—is out of the question. Kissing, fellatio, all must be weighed. The tree of sex shrivels up. When I go to the Jewel in New York, or the baths in Jacksonville, I see what I've come to call the Same Nine People. They're not exactly nine, and they're not always the same, but almost, and you get the point. The fact is, there does not have to be a lot of Patient Zeros out there to destroy the way of life we had evolved; there just has to be one. As long as a friend writes me from San Diego that a man he knows in an AZT program out there called to ask him if he had any ethyl chloride for the march in Washington, because he thought it the greatest cruising opportunity ever—well, that's enough.

One afternoon last spring we took a walk down to the Morton Street pier and found a wire-mesh fence along its perimeter to keep people away from the rotting timbers at the edge. Not in New York, of course: There were still people sunbathing along the margin, beyond the concrete divider and the silver fence. One in particular was nude; the sun gleamed on every pore of his bare back and buttocks, the tiny hairs on his forearm and neck—and I stood there for a moment staring at him, wondering which one of us was confined. The nude and the chicken wire fence was one of those images that expresses the whole dilemma. Or the nude and the Plexiglas panel, in the bookstore off Times Square a friend of mine repairs to after an exhausting day at work—the individual booths are all separated by transparent walls, like a handball court one can see into, and the men stand in their separate cells, jerking off to one another. Or the dance floor at Track's. It's filled with people dancing; the handsome men take their shirts off at a certain point, as they used to formerly, observing rituals practiced by a court that no longer exists. It is all muted, a ghost of itself, all difficult to explain, till I see a muscular man beating a stick against a gourd while a woman dances to his syncopation and, as she whirls around, read what the sweatshirt she's wearing says: CHOOSE LIFE. That is the caption that explains the dance now, and our whole community. You've heard of postmodern. This is post-trust.

The Absence of Anger

"Y OURE NOT ANGRY yet. You don't feel the gun at your head," says the man who has taken the podium after a series of speakers have addressed the crowd at the community center on Thirteenth Street. He looks out at them and says this in the calm, slightly amazed voice of someone who has seen the symptoms of apathy so many times he can perceive them even through wild applause—in this case, the wild applause of a room filled with people seated on every available chair, bench, ledge, and shelf and standing in the back corners on tiptoe to see and hear the speakers who have gone before. "You just don't feel the gun at your head," he repeats, almost to himself, in amazement, in a sort of dream voice, marveling. He surveys them for a moment with a smile on his lips, a smile of wonder and, perhaps, condescension and amusement—from the height of his own anger, his own suffering, his own knowledge of what it does feel like to have the gun barrel on his temple, that is, to have AIDS. "What will it take? What will it take to make you angry?"

In truth, of course, nobody knows. He does not know. Nor, even worse, does the audience—the people who have just been asked the question. They were, at the outset of the first speech, asked to stand if they had or knew someone who has AIDS. Most did. They were asked again to stand up—in every other row of folding chairs, starting from the first—and told, once they were on their feet: "That's how many of you will not be here in five years." And later: "By 1992, half of the people in this room will be dead." Why then, aren't they angry? Why *don't* they feel the gun is at their heads?

I have come here wondering exactly that—I feel I should be angry, and I'm not—though the fact that I'm late getting here for the meeting, and the reason I'm late getting here for the meeting, provides me already with a partial answer. The reason I'm late is that I was having dinner with a friend who is sick with AIDS and did not want to rush off after coffee because I do not know when I'll see him again (I am leaving New York tomorrow), and because I did not want to tell him I was going to a meeting he is probably too weak to attend, since he must conserve his strength for the six flights of stairs he must climb to and from his loft every time he goes out. That is one reason I am not angry, I guess—anger is subsumed, lost, in sadness. It did not even seem a matter of choice—being with E. was far more important than arriving on time for a political meeting. Sorrow, moreover, is a sort of immobilizing emotion. It requires stillness, removal, withdrawal from the world. We sat in the dark loft while the Four Last Songs of Strauss played (*How can he bear this?* I wondered) and talked about books, friends, fate, as we watched the city sky darken and the lighted towers of Wall Street become sharp as diamonds. (It is exactly this the activists protest against: our turning philosophical when we should be angry. And it is exactly the opposite the gay men organizing home care for people with AIDS accuse the activists of: playing politics when they should be sitting at bedsides.) Eventually I left—slowly; as if I had nothing to do afterward, as if I were not leaving him by himself—and ran uptown to this meeting already in progress, the friend (whose speech I'd come to hear) already speaking. And, like a concertgoer who arrives after the start of a symphony, I wait in the hall. Beside me the black lesbian security guard is talking to two men in yarmulkes about a woman in Brooklyn with AIDS. On the bulletin board are the notices and advertisements endemic to universities everywhere that are still associated with the sixties—that changeless universe of yoga classes, guitar lessons, marches on Washington, shares in an apartment, requests for a room—including one that reads, "Two leather men, one from Argentina, one from Amsterdam, need place to stay in Chelsea. Close to bars, with room for weight-lifting equipment." Such a duo would have set hearts thumping in the seventies; now they remind me of that Polish ship that arrived ten days too late for the Bicentennial celebration. Times have changed, fellas. One no longer wants to be close to bars. One comes instead to places like the community center, the old Firehouse born out of its ashes, the sixties coming back relentlessly to life, like some mummy in a horror film. There is nothing quite so depressing as the doctrine of eternal recurrence. One wants to go up to people on Saint Marks Place with long hair and headbands, take them by the shoulders and say, "Don't you know all this has been *done?*" Which is why even this—the call for demonstrations—seems like one more dreary consequence of AIDS, and why it may have fallen on indifferent ears; like the ads for yoga class, the clutter of this bulletin board, the anger of the speakers inside, it merely seems something out of the past that has just been wound up again, like an old Victrola.

The trouble is, of course, that there may be reasonable cause, now, for anger—just how reasonable is what I've come to this place to find out. A certain bitterness comes easily already. It is easy to be angry with God, or the virus, or the general arrangement of the universe in which a microbe takes man from the summit, the apex, of mammalian life to the nadir of bacterial existence, which changes him from a paragon a little lower than the angels to the doormat of every germ that comes through the door; nature's punching bag. It is easy to be disgusted by the fact that the same phenomenon that caused Rice-A-Roni to drop its jingle ("The San Francisco Treat") apparently kept President Reagan from even saying the word AIDS till only recently: AIDS does not sell political programs or noodles. Even the most apathetic citizen cannot help but compare the government's response to AIDS with its reaction—speedy, alarmed, passionate—to a disease contracted by Legionnaires having a convention at a hotel in Philadelphia during the seventies. But one is also cynical enough to realize the ramifications of the fact that AIDS is *not* spread by an air conditioner at a hotel occupied by a convention of Legionnaires. AIDS is spread by sex; in America, sex among homosexuals. And needles; needles used by drug addicts. That queer quartet that introduced the subject of AIDS to North America—Haitians, homosexuals, hemophiliacs, and heroin addicts—has never really left the minds of most Americans, no matter how many people not in those categories have died since then. Forget the babies, receivers of blood transfusions, African heterosexuals—it is still a gay disease, and as it moves into the black and Hispanic ghettos of the northern cities (those apparent pools of excess humanity mainstream America can see no role for besides breakdancing and rap music), AIDS solidifies itself as divine eugenics—that forbidden science Hitler was the last to try, that lurking fantasy people still harbor ("If only the human race, the population of this corrupt world, could be *edited*"). And so there is no national pressure to solve the problem, so long as it remains within these communities. The resources of the entire nation have not been marshaled because the entire nation has not been threatened; AIDS remains the problem of a special-interest group, in the eyes of conservatives, who, like Robert Novak on the television program *Crossfire*, suggest gays *hope* straight people will contract AIDS, so they can get more funding.

This is indeed politics at its most cynical, but no doubt in their heart of hearts, Hispanic drug addicts who abandon their babies with AIDS and homosexual activists are not exactly people America *wants* within its borders. A few years ago William Safire suggested that homosexuals simply remain invisible, and that is probably the consensus still. By now homosexuals have become accustomed to the idea that there are people who would like to see them simply subtracted from society. Including the religious. The early Christians were shocked by the custom of exposing unwanted babies in the marketplace or on the roadside in ancient Rome—to die of exposure, unless someone picked them up, and took them home—but one cannot help but see a different instinct in some of their descendants. The house-burning in Arcadia, Florida, the treatment of schoolchildren like Ryan White, is just part of the urge to keep the victims of AIDS outside the community, the home, the school, the marketplace, to wither away alone. Homosexuals rebelled against nature, and now nature is taking its revenge, wrote Pat Buchanan—before he was hired by the White House as its communications director. It is a view that allows those willing to brand homosexuals lepers the instant they had an excuse for doing so, to write off a portion of the human race in a vast collective hiss of "I told you so." Why? Because AIDS is not caused by an air conditioner in Philadelphia; AIDS is transmitted through sex. Famine gets rock stars to hold benefits, but no one packs stadiums because Africans are dying in even greater numbers of AIDS.

But even this malice isn't enough to make most homosexuals angry—this hysteria and hatred are things most of them are long familiar with. When the brother of a conservative activist takes an ad out in the *Washington Post* to say the deceased activist was not homosexual and, while dying, reconciled himself with the Church by repenting his past (like the lawyer who defends his client by saying not only was his client not in the hotel that night, but if so, he did not assault the waiter), they shake their heads and smile a bitter smile. What lengths, what depths, people will go to in their aversion! Ditto the obituaries that refuse to list AIDS as the cause of death—as if there were only one thing worse than being dead and that is being homosexual. The high-pitched giggle Pat Buchanan broke into whenever interviewing a homosexual on *Crossfire*—the blush, the expression of a nine-year-old boy telling a dirty joke that inevitably suffused his face, the near falsetto of his voice when homosexuality was the subject of the program—only typifies the way legions of people like him view homosexuals: as an off-color joke. Homosexuals, I suspect, *expected* the length of time it took the president to even say the word *AIDS* in public, considered it part of the way things are, something they had and would always have to live with. And there was something else—

AIDS had also induced a kind of shock—a numbness—those first few years; the sense of unreality that occurs to us when our car begins to spin on a patch of ice or collide with another vehicle. *What is going on?* That is the chief question. One is not angry. One is dumbfounded.

Of course *all* these questions that come under the heading of "Why aren't you angry?"—Why do homosexuals not have elected leaders? Why do they not support a national organization? Why do they not employ a lobby in Washington to further their interests? Why do they not donate to gay candidates?—had been around long before AIDS. They were one of the perplexing enigmas that followed the Stonewall rebellion. Why had liberation largely expressed itself as promiscuity?

Well, for one thing, homosexuality is about sex. Most animals wish to be alone when they lay their eggs. It's hard to base a political platform on what one does behind closed doors—or in the toilets of subways. For another, homosexuality is for the most part invisible. If blacks have no choice in the matter, homosexuals could pass; and did so. The perfectly natural desire to conduct one's private life in private—an instinct common to everyone—in this case contravenes the need to stand up and be counted; and show the rest of society how average, random, and like everyone else most homosexuals are. Who wanted to be a target? Who wanted to be a lightning rod for the hatred of people from Pat Buchanan to the thug on the street who, in the company of six other adolescents, went looking for gays to bash? Life was too short to waste precious time on goons. The easiest way to be homosexual was to be homosexual in private—that's where one's homosexuality occurred, anyway. And so the attempts, long before AIDS arrived, to gather the tribe together, to consolidate money, support, political clout, collided with the universal desire to keep one's sexual life as private as everyone else's. As Freud said years ago, "Homosexuality is no vice, Madame, but assuredly no advantage."

And let us not forget that homosexuals *are* like most people and, like most people, indifferent to politics and loathe to burn tires in the streets. The percentage of politically militant homosexuals is probably the same in every generation and probably the same in the general population—a fervent few. Political agitation is simply a vocation few people have in life; and those who have it are always asking, How can we get everyone else off their butts? Complicating the picture is no doubt another fact: Some homosexuals disapprove of their homosexual self. That self-repudiation is something that has never been addressed fully in gay life; it may lie beneath so many layers of apparently well-adapted behavior that the problem of people who have counted themselves out on some deep level, lowered their ambitions, stayed away from arenas in which they felt they could not succeed, is similar perhaps to that of blacks. No one even sees the self-hatred. They take William Safire's advice to simply keep quiet. And finally, even the homosexual population has its common selfishness; Scott Fitzgerald's description of the man who cares not if the whole world crashes down so long as it spares his own house applies here. *Let me just hide till all this is over,* people think, *smear blood upon the door, and let the Angel of Death pass over this house.* And so anger has been lost in a general withdrawal—an attempt to escape the general fate.

That is, the virus was just the latest in a series of diseases that no amount of money or research seems able to cure; as horrible and implacable as muscular dystrophy, multiple sclerosis, Parkinson's, Alzheimer's, Lou Gehrig's disease. In short, not all the anger or all the money in the world could eliminate these blights on human health—we had to wait for some accident, some breakthrough, some genius in a laboratory that might or might not be one of those funded by the government. We had to wait for an apple to fall on Newton's head; for Archimedes to shout "Eureka!"

And so, despite the charge by Larry Kramer that the incompetence, stupidity, and bureaucratic paralysis of the government-medical establishment amounted to genocide —that homosexuals are this generation's Jews being led off to the showers—there was little anger against the government. The government was considered just the government, not helpful to gay men but not conspiring to murder them either, coldly and consciously, that is. Most people are simply not conspiracy-minded; most people do not believe this is genocide. If San Francisco surpassed New York immeasurably in the care and treatment of AIDS patients, San Francisco had always surpassed New York in everything having to do with issues of gay life. But most homosexuals did not think Mayor Koch was Hitler. Most homosexuals, in fact, turned away from the public arena altogether and made this a personal matter. Sickness usually is. As in: Why did I let this happen to me? The anger was just a "God damn it," directed under one's breath, on walks late at night, against fate; this fate that has no favorites, intercedes never on our behalf, merely unfolds. If one was angry, one was angry at the virus—this dumb, lifeless, blind, greedy microbe that was so stupid it killed the very thing it fed on, reproducing itself to no purpose. And, no doubt, one was angry with oneself. Because in searching for the answer to that question, "Why aren't you angry?" it would be wrong to overlook one of the most bizarre things about accidents (like AIDS)—that people to whom they happen blame themselves, as if bad luck were a moral failing. Nothing is so difficult for the human mind to accept as the fact that much suffering in life is random, meaningless, and in a sense completely trivial: the wrong place at the wrong time. Once the plague established itself, gay men in doctors' offices all over Manhattan were weeping over their pasts. AIDS had simply tapped into the remorse, the conviction ("I have been unlucky in life") harbored by homosexuals who may not even suspect they have these feelings. Echoing Pat Buchanan, they say, "If only I had not been homosexual, this never would have happened." Strictly true, perhaps. But their being homosexual did not cause the illness; the virus simply exploited their homosexuality. But like someone whose child is injured on a hike they took them on, they blame themselves for ever having gone walking.

And so, as with victims of rape or any misfortune, gay men have been silenced by a peculiar guilt induced by the misfortune—which makes the minority who have formed organizations, raised money, prodded the government, gone on television to educate others, defended themselves against the Pat Buchanans and Robert Novaks and Jerry Falwells, all the more admirable. The fact that gay men did not throw rocks, set cars on fire, or besiege the White House was chiefly because they did other things that seemed more constructive at the time. They did march on Washington, they did print newspapers, they did criticize elected politicians. They did picket the airlines when Northwest refused to fly a sick man back from the Orient because he had AIDS. It is a long battle ahead, after all, and it will be necessary, of course, to confront this sort of unacceptable behavior each time it occurs. The fact is that in some curious way, though the people in this room have been told flat out that half of them will be dead in five years, none of them knows what else he can do about it—except for what he has already done. And because, most curious of all, most odd, most marvelous, the truth is none of them is really chilled by the assertion—each of them thinks he will escape, I suspect. As Freud also said, "No one really believes in his own death."

Ties

THE EVENING OF December 3, 1983,
it rained hard in Manhattan, and yet I couldn't stay in my
apartment—I had been living in a house in the suburbs
all fall, where one stays indoors and things come to you
(United Parcel, mailmen, relatives with day-old dough-
nuts). The chance to be out walking through the streets
was intoxicating, even in the rain, even at the end of a
rotten year, in the early-winter darkness. The year 1983
seemed to be a year of blows: the circumstances compelling
me to leave town in September and now the funeral of a
friend dead of AIDS that brought me back. If—before I
left—I was like most residents of Manhattan, who lead,
despite the cliché, lives as routine as people in small towns,
I now found myself walking east from the Astor Place
subway at five o'clock with the surge of adrenaline that
affects tourists and the happiness of a traveler finally returning home. Home was the little hole-in-the-wall that
sells Middle Eastern food to go, which was the first thing
that brought me to a halt near the corner of Saint Marks
Place and Third Avenue. Waiting for the Arab to finish
stuffing the pita bread for the woman on my left, things
looked the way they did to Emily in *Our Town* when she
comes back to earth as a ghost because she misses her old
life: Everything was poignant, as I waited for the Arab to
toast my pita. An actor from the Negro Ensemble Com-

pany came up and said to the woman standing next to me that he'd been assured he would be in the production they had just auditioned for, and as they talked happy actors' talk, I thought, *Isn't this just how someone imagines New York? You wait for the Arab to give you your pita sandwich while two ecstatic young actors talk about their next show, while beyond the awning the rain is streaming down in slanting orange lines and all these people are coming home from their day uptown to romantic little apartments in the East Village.* Was this rain real? Or were we shooting a film? There was a functioning dry telephone in my apartment just a few doors away, but the street, the crowds, the excitement of being here again were so intense I went next to the bank of pay phones near Second Avenue and started making my calls there. The handsome man who came up to use the phone on my left intensified the romantic element—who is he? who's he calling?—as the faces went past in the rain and I found myself listening, in a few seconds, to a friend tell me he'd quit his job in August, gone to Greece and Paris, nursed his lover through hepatitis, changed his apartment, and wanted me to come to dinner that evening to meet the young man his roommate was "interviewing" as a possible boyfriend.

When you leave New York and come back, the joke is you find nothing has changed—despite the infinite number of trivial events—but this time I learned a lot had: Not only had friends left their jobs or moved to new apartments, but most of them were depressed—one newly macrobiotic and saintly; another living half of each week in the country; another visiting doctors who told him to calm down; another who was asked to come back for a blood test. Returning after four months, I was like the relative of a patient recuperating in a hospital, or a parent who visits his child in school infrequently: One arrives and expects to see progress. You want to see your patient better, walking again, your child fluent in French, your city cured of the plague. But apparently there is no cure for this plague. There are things being tried—so many that one man who died said before he went, "The treatment is worse than the disease"—but the friend whose funeral I was here to attend had tried most of them. For that was why I was back—to attend the funeral of Eddie, a friend so bound up with New York it was hard to imagine the city without him, a friend who so unfailingly enjoyed everything that was new in New York—from nightclubs to phone systems to winter coats—even now I had the impression he'd got AIDS only because he was always the first to do everything.

Eddie's motto, in fact, if he had one, was that of Auntie Mame, his favorite heroine: "Life is a banquet and most poor fools are starving to death." Not Eddie. Long past the point at which most people I knew had begun to slow down—to stay home on Saturday nights with Sunday's *New York Times,* to stop going to Fire Island, to stop dancing (unless it was what one friend replied when I asked him where he was dancing these days: "In my living room!"), to stop going out to new clubs ("I've been to all the night-clubs," one said, "including the ones that haven't opened yet."), to stop participating in the sixty things each night that made living in Manhattan distinct from living in, say, Rutland, Vermont. Eddie kept going. Eddie was out every night. He was in fact whatever you call the man who stands in front of certain nightclubs and decides who will get in and who won't. His life was nocturnal—he got home around four or five in the morning and then, if he hadn't arranged to have one of the bouncers from Brooklyn come over ("Let me put it this way—he has no neck"), he slept. For only four or five hours; like Napoleon, Eddie got by on less than most of us need. And then, from the depths of that eccentric apartment we'd christened the Eighth Wonder of the World, he awoke and began to telephone; depositing the details of the night before, the incidents, the shoes, the faces, the celebrities, into my ear as if I were the diary he was too busy, too excited, to keep.

He knew where to go in the East Village for a Shiatsu massage, and where to go near Times Square for male strip shows, and where to go on lower Broadway for the cowboy boots and shirts he began buying after he and a friend returned from the gay rodeo in Reno. He had a pass to Man's Country—the baths we both frequented— and passes to three or four fashion shows a day when the collections were being shown. His dream was to go around the world on the *QE2* as a member of the crew assigned to dine and dance with widows from Omaha traveling alone. Instead he went to the dentist one day and learned he had tumors on his gums—tumors he showed me one day when they were larger and we were walking down Fifth Avenue in the bright sunlight on our way to go shopping. "Do you want to see them?" he said and then pulled his upper lip back so they were visible: dark purple, like clusters of grapes.

Eddie was not embarrassed by anything personal; he began to tell the people he met, "I have cancer, but I'm not going to die," in the same breathless, dramatic voice he used to describe the arrival of the king of Spain at Studio 54. And he telephoned every morning with the same cheer to tell me not only that he'd fainted in the hospital elevator the previous afternoon but that "that gorgeous boy we used to say had a Very Important Stomach—the one who plays *base*ball, you know—came to my interferon group today, only they gave him too much and he was shaking like a windshield wiper. Covered with spots!" His spots went away when he was radiated; then they came back; still, we listened to the progress of his illness with a certain impatience, a certain refusal to take it in—like children who cannot allow a parent to get sick. Eddie after all was the central figure in our family of friends—New York itself, somehow. When a man got on the elevator we were riding in one afternoon at the D&D Building and asked politely, "How are you?" and Eddie said, "I have cancer," another friend of ours turned to Eddie after the man—speechless, shocked—got off at the next floor and said, "Couldn't you say you've been swimming *laps?*" For we somehow could not permit him to be ill. And that was the only change in Eddie's appearance we could see: a certain gauntness. Eddie claimed, "It's in the eyes. I can tell, in any crowd, at any party, who has It. It's in the eyes." And so, just the way he'd told us about Los Angeles—how they dressed, what the houses were like—and the rodeo in Reno, the crowd at Studio, the models in Kenzo's fashion show, so Eddie became the first traveler to a new and scary destination.

There was a white high-rise building about halfway between Eddie's apartment on Fifth Avenue and mine in the East Village—a building occupied primarily, it seemed, by elderly Jewish men and women who were often being wheeled up and down the sidewalk by maids from the Caribbean when I walked by. Across the street from them was a small school playground behind a chicken wire fence and a churchyard in which apple trees bloomed in spring. I left New York not long after Eddie began treatments for his tumors; he would, with the enthusiasm and interest he had shown all his life for what was new and experimental try anything—things we learned later had probably hastened his death. The next time I came back to New York on a visit, Eddie looked like one of the eighty-year-old Jewish men watching the children play kickball from his wheelchair across the street. He was dressed in a black overcoat and scarf, though it was a warm spring day; his face was even gaunter, and the flesh around his mouth seemed to protrude to make room for the tumors; he shuffled along at the pace very old people, who are usually in a wheelchair, use. We walked from the lunch he served at his apartment—he loved to cook for his friends, and only afterward did we learn he was careless about what he himself ate—to a store on University Place that rented videocassettes. He was bringing some movies back and he did so very slowly. He rented both conventional and pornographic films, and he took me to the shelves of cassettes to tell me which ones he'd rented (*"Teen Marine* is fabulous!") and select new ones. When we left the store, the people behind us finally could wait no longer and veered around him, like cars passing on a highway. Eddie only smiled as I waited on the sidewalk outside for him to finally cross the threshold. Smiled at their impatience, his own predicament. We parted on that corner; I thanked him for lunch and did not look back till I had crossed the street—to see him standing there, turning north to start his long shuffle back to his apartment, a man of forty in a heavy black overcoat and scarf on a warm spring day who happened to look ninety-five.

The friends whose mascot he had always been were faithful to him; one gave me news on the phone of how he was doing—the naps he took every day at five, a sudden blindness, his discovery of classical music. *Teen Marine* was beyond him now. He began listening to Mozart. That was how I—five hundred miles to the west that winter, taking a walk each night in the only place available, a local cemetery illumined by the lights of a nearby shopping mall—thought of Eddie: lying in the Eighth Wonder, blind, listening to Mozart. One Saturday morning the word came that relieved the strain, the knowledge of his suffering and the suffering itself. "Some private-duty nurse they hired called his brother at four in the morning," said the friend. "She wanted to know where her check was, Eddie was dead. Can you believe it? Eddie's gone, dear. Eddie's gone. He took a left."

That was the problem, as I stood there now on the sidewalk of a city that seemed inseparable from his voice each morning on the phone. One might as well say New York was finished. In fact everything remained, just as I remembered it—even the baths on my block whose two slender black doors people were going in and out of as I stood there watching. "There's no reason to go to New York anymore," two British art critics said in an article I'd read on the plane about the fall season in various capitals, "now that sex and drugs are Out." Try telling New Yorkers that, I thought. Ah New York! Ah humanity! It is banal by now to say the whorehouses in Paris were never as busy as they were during the plague. But when I went into the baths to sit in its cafeteria for a while, before the wake began— it seemed the right restaurant, in this case—I watched men passing the doorway in their towels who looked exactly as they did before the world turned upside down. The music in fact was wonderfully familiar—a flawless blend of the best songs of the seventies that made me very sentimental; Eddie and I had danced to some of them. Listening to "You're My Peace of Mind" as the men walked by, I thought, *The faces, the music,* were *wondrous—still are—and the fact that some virus has insinuated itself into the collective bloodstream through the promiscuity that homosexual life evolved is a medical, not a moral, fact.*

Or was it? I wasn't sure. Eddie was dead either way, and I left the warm cafeteria and its amazing view without touching the men we used to gasp over together (the central expression of our friendship: the gasp) and walked down Saint Marks Place to the funeral home. The funeral home was only a block from the baths. (In another case, they were side by side.) The men gathering at the chapel in their dark suits and ties were even handsomer than those I'd seen pass the doorway at the baths—men I was used to seeing in towels or bathing suits, in fact, or beach clothes on a sunny boardwalk. The rabbi—a whirling dervish on

the dance floor one summer—speaks of a special generation that is being singled out, afflicted before its time. It
seems wrong that the pleasure we shared should lead to
death—it seems out of proportion to the crime; but, then,
this is a medical, not a moral fact. I feel numb and unreal
in the little chapel. I have not taken a full breath since
entering; the air is heavier here, oppressive, weighty, and
thick. This is not happening, I think. This is not the reason
we gather together. These are the people Eddie has adored
all these years—and *adored* is the correct word. These are
the people whose beauty he praised, whose style he appreciated, whose exploits he followed, whose friend he
finally became. These are the men who—handsome, bright,
successful, original—constituted the glamour Eddie, and
New York, was so fond of. They do not gather together
for this. They come together for parties, for beaches, for
dinner, for fun—for a song that Eddie used to drag me
out of the house to run down to the bar to hear. ("The
one where the violins keep going up, up, up!") But there
is the casket being wheeled down the aisle, through the
dense, airless room. There are Eddie's parents—this col-
lision of Eddie's two worlds, his past and his present—in
the midst of these men, and there is Martin delivering the
eulogy to a crowd Eddie would have loved, for they have
all turned out for him. Only he isn't here to describe their
faces, and their shoes, and their love affairs; he isn't here
to whisper, "Look at that man with the puffed lips, and
those aristocratic hands! He's *drop-dead!*" So's Eddie. And
when we pour outside onto the street afterward, the dark-
ening streets, the red sky above the rooftops, the sidewalks
thronged with people coming home from work—all seem
to demand his presence, or at least his comments on the
funeral we have just attended. The odd thing about a wake
is it leaves you feeling very alive afterward. "Who was that
handsome man with the beard in the third row?" says a

friend, supplying words that Eddie would have otherwise; it's the first sign that life goes on. The funeral is reviewed: shoes, beards, friends, strangers. We walk down Second Avenue together in the suits and ties we rarely wear in each other's presence and enter a café. The café is warm, crowded with young men and women who sit in black turtlenecks writing in their journals, like the Hollywood version of an artists' café. We find a table. We notice the man behind the counter making carrot juice has beautiful forearms. A friend tells the story of the oboe player from Minneapolis who came to live with him this summer. Everyone at the table agrees a favorite male model looked wonderful and that Eddie would have loved the crowd who came to his wake. The carrot cake, hot chocolate, and tea arrive, the room gets louder, handsome young men come into the café. Happy to be here, with his three friends— the tourist suddenly takes their four neckties and joins them at their tips over the tea and coffee cups in the center of the table. He doesn't know why he does this; it seems a silly gesture; he suspected the differences in the four neckties might reveal something about each of them, or he wants to unite the quartet at that moment, somehow. When he sees it does not and no one understands what he is doing, he returns them to their shirt fronts and goes on talking about the funeral, watching the people in the room with a wild eagerness, thinking it is still the most extraordinary city, lovely, horrendous, thrilling, sad. And missing one thing, besides sex and drugs: Eddie.

Stars

WALKING IS CONSIDERED odd in this little town in the country—but since the laying of a sidewalk last summer, you can go all the way uptown now to the intersection where two highways crisscross each other beneath a traffic light, before the facade of a gas station, a fried-chicken franchise, and a stretch of railroad tracks. The intersection could be anywhere in the United States, anywhere at all, but on the way, you walk past particular things: the insurance agency, the nursery that failed last year in the freeze, the bank, the town hall, and the public park. In the park is a fountain that plashes in the still night for apparently nobody's benefit but my own; at night I am usually the only person out. Sometimes the lights are on above the tennis courts, and people are playing a game or are on the basketball court adjacent to the courts, shooting baskets. Sometimes I make out a solitary teenage boy dribbling a basketball in the dark (the lights now cost twenty-five cents every half hour; in the old days people walked away and left them burning) with the radio on in his car to keep him company. There is also a man who walks his poodle on a leash in his pajamas, and sometimes a policeman is sitting in his car by the public beach waiting for a crime to be committed. Twice I have been accused of a crime—most recently, a woman saw someone walk across her lawn, phoned the cops, and they stopped me and asked to see my footprints. (To take a walk in the United States is to be suspected either of poverty or criminal intent.) Sometimes it is overcast, and in the summer often too humid, but in winter it is mostly clear and dry, and when you finally go up the hill past the public beach and begin the last stretch along the dark, silent gardens of the houses on the lake, you are all alone beneath a cloudless sky. The stars in Florida in the winter are mesmerizing—though it may be merely my imagination, they seem more thickly strewn across the sky than in the summer. Or perhaps the cool air merely leaves one free to look up at them undisturbed—no bugs to swat, no heat to make you want to get indoors to a ceiling fan or air conditioner. In winter, conditions for starwatching are perfect; the stars are plenteous and bright, and, if there isn't any moon, you stand there looking up with the distinct feeling that you are on the surface of a planet suspended in space shared by countless others that merely face you, like houses across the lake.

In a small town at night a walk clears the head, gets you out of the house, lets your mind wander, sets you free. I am upset when I meet someone else walking; I have grown accustomed to having the sidewalk to myself as I let unravel in the darkness whatever is on my mind, so that, returning an hour later, whatever facts, events, incidents have made that day good or bad seem to have played themselves out and become a little more ordered than they were on first receiving them. Sometimes I leave the house after a telephone call from New York. I digest the news—so dense with incident—in the silence exuded by the sleeping gardens. Sometimes the news is bad: a friend is sick, or dead. Tonight I'm told a man committed suicide rather than suffer any longer the deterioration caused by the virus. On the tennis courts I see two couples playing, and some kids on the basketball court beyond, borrowing their light, and the first thing I think about them is, *They do not have*

It. It has nothing to do with them. The stars are very white above me when I put the tennis courts behind and go down the hill by the public beach, very thick and beautiful in the black sky—and I think, *R. belongs to that now, a part again of the universe, no longer in human form, a mix of elements, vaporized, cremated, gone, eternal, and dissembled: as unearthly as a star.* And he joins a constellation not marked in the maps of the heavens—of these friends and acquaintances who have now entered the past; I imagine them all out there, white pinpoints of light, stars.

Some of them were stars—to me, or the homosexual world of New York City, or the world in general. Some of them were men who were famous for designing clothes or buildings, or interpreting history, or composing music. Some of them were merely admired on Fire Island. Some were stars in pornographic films—like the man I saw in the slides flashed on the screen of a bar in Washington several years ago, one of the sexual icons of New York, who was in fact withering away even as the men around me paused in the conversation, their drinking, to admire his penis and his pectorals. And now this most recent, newest star: a man so good-looking everyone urged him to become a model, but who chose to remain in publishing, a copywriter, a man from California whose skin, hair, teeth, smile, and bright good looks were startling on the gray streets of Manhattan, whose grime and falling dust could not dim his blondness. He was so blond that is what I remember, and unlike everyone else I knew of that hue—whose appearance was affected by age, stress, fast living, the general ash of the urban air—he looked as crisp and golden the last time I saw him as he did the day ten years before when we first met. His Western health was a kind of marvel. Why didn't the city get to him? He lived in a house with friends, and former lovers, in the city and commuted to Fire Island in the summers; he was a staple, an icon, of homosexual

New York City—handsome but not vain, smart but not mean, blond but not wasted; so that when he got sick, we were all shocked as if it had never happened before, and when he killed himself, we felt a light had been extinguished—and a new star put up in the sky, beneath which I walk on these quiet nights with fear, dread, remorse, sadness, and disgust in the heart. Fear, of It. Dread: Who's next? Remorse: that we should have lived differently. Sadness: that friends suffered. Disgust: that something common as the flu, wretched as African pestilence, could destroy so much that was secure, beautiful, happy; that there should be such penalties for sex. I look at the public beach as I walk by—in a ravine, where a stream issues from another lake. I see a dark grove of live oaks draped with Spanish moss swaying in the breeze, a pale white dock and changing room whose white clapboard sides gleam in the streetlight refracted through the limbs of the trees—and want only one thing: to be alive, and able to swim when the weather gets warm this coming summer.

This ambition is somewhat scaled down from previous ones: I used to take this walk wondering if I should get in the car and drive to Jacksonville and visit the baths and bars. I felt on the loveliest nights—when the moon was new, and there was a soft, warm breeze, and the sensations that characterize a Southern Night were all in bloom—that such beauty, such a night, required a lover. Then I felt sorry for myself, annoyed that homosexual life was confined to cities, and in those cities to one-night stands. Now I have no such ambitions, do not demand a lover, merely want life. A decrease in expectations, the economists would call it; a rise in conservatism, the politicians; a return to morality, the priests. In fact it is fear and loathing; in reality it is the mind scrambling to accommodate itself to facts beyond its control. The town seems to me as exotic as a colony on the moon because it does not have it. The little old lady who sits alone in her tiny living room in the miniature house so near the sidewalk I can almost reach in through the window and touch her; the solitary adolescent dribbling his basketball on the cement court in the darkness, his bare chest flashing as he passes near the faint radiance of the streetlight; the children who have left their tricycles tilted in the sand of their driveway might as well be living on another planet—and as I walk past the bank whose sign flashes the time and temperature with a loud *clunk*, I feel I can deal with only two facts: *It is nine forty-three, it is sixty-three degrees.* That is all I want to know right now. I don't want any more phone calls, any more news —I have come to detest the sound of a ringing phone.

This shrinking—of the universe to a bank sign on this quiet night—while above me the eerie stars provoke dreary thoughts, this reduction of my dreams to the simple goal of being able to swim this summer, intensifies as the roll call of expiring men expands. As every other day the television or newspaper carries some new fact—300,000 are exposed, Dr. Curran announces; 30,000 will get It in the next five years—one's desires, defiance, beliefs, wilt. One wonders if there isn't some way to fight back—besides celibacy, that is; a treatment of some kind that would allow one to go out and meet the barbarians rather than sit quietly in fear waiting for them to reach the gate. "It's so depressing," a friend says on the phone from New York, after telling me about his arrangements to increase his insurance and make out a will. "You mean all this grown-up stuff," I say. "No," he says, "I mean all this death stuff."

This death stuff is unnerving—one gets up each day, or walks through the quiet town at night, past the two-story houses with lights burning in cozy rooms, and dogs drooping on porches, and bicycles knocked over in the sand, and wonders just how many more facts one will have to absorb. When will it happen? Where do I want to be when it does?

How will it happen? Friends say if you don't want to get it, you won't; but this seems to me silly; friends who did not want to die have. Your desire to live one, two, three, or four years is within your power, to a degree; but how much more? And you wonder as you walk through the sleeping town under a sky filled with crystalline stars how this happened, because on quiet nights in winter you have time to think over the past fifteen years and ask, *Could I have lived differently? Been a different kind of homosexual?*

Even as I do, a friend of mine ten years younger is living in the apartment above the first one I lived in, in New York, and writing me letters at three in the morning about the men he has just met, and in some cases slept with—and I thrill to this reenactment of the adventure I had when I moved to the city, and think happily, *It still goes on.* Yet I wonder if this vicarious pleasure is not foolish. In Florida as of February there are thirty-five new cases a month. Thirty thousand are predicted over the next five years in the nation. Promiscuity is, after all, like the engine of some giant ocean liner, which takes days to start once it is stopped. Promiscuity is so huge, so enormous, so habitual, so vital that it is brought to a halt very slowly, and only in the direst of circumstances: the equation of death with sex. There are homosexuals who say promiscuity is our right and cannot be taken away from us, but this sounds like the man on the bridge screaming he has a right to jump. Shut the whole vast machine down, with a shudder, and let us be quiet till this thing is trapped. Because each evening I take this walk, it is pure sentimentality to imagine friends who have disappeared as stars twinkling in the night sky above the earth—in fact they are just gone.

And the statue to be erected in Sheridan Square of two men on a bench seems oddly outdated now—perhaps a piece of marble with names engraved on it might make more sense. The town beneath these stars does not remember how blond, bright, witty, and well liked R. was; nor does the woman behind the counter of the Seven-Eleven store across the railroad tracks whose bright light brings me in out of the darkness. It is open all night. Inside, the woman who works the register on the graveyard shift is talking to a customer buying Tootsie Rolls about a city they have both lived in: San Diego. I buy some cookies, and a wrestling magazine that features foldouts of ten wrestling stars who, both hairy and smooth-chested, wear elaborate belt buckles, tattoos, black bathing suits. It is the sort of magazine a ten-year-old boy might buy or a girl who follows the wrestlers on TV, I guess—neither of which I am, or both of which I am, as I walk home with the magazine folded in my pocket, feeling like a kid who hopes to grow up and have enormous muscles. I guess I still do. Walking home with my cookies, my wrestler magazine, the sound of my footsteps down the quiet street, I have regressed; I might as well be ten; my desires as chaste as stars. And soon I have left the light behind, and pass the boy still dribbling his basketball with an intensity that sounds odd in the deep darkness but comes no doubt from the fact that as he leaps up to make his shot, he too imagines he's a star. Down in the hollow, coming up from the beach, I think the real stars at this moment are the journalists, scientists, volunteers in New York and San Francisco, and wherever else, caring for the men determined to hang on to their human form. And the doctor who delivers us from this thing the brightest star of all. But enough of metaphors. Now the real stars make me stop on the sidewalk and look up: so cold and brilliant, so far away, so unlike anything we know. All that remains beneath them on this planet of hope and dread is the determination to remain terrestrial. All that beats in the stillness of the winter night is the basketball, and the horrified heart.

Oceans

"THERE HAS TO be a beach at the end of this," a friend said. There was a beach at the beginning, certainly—the one in Brazil, Hawaii, Mexico people went to when the plague began and they thought they could escape it by simply going elsewhere; the sex-vacation. The sex-vacation is no more. One might—like the Spaniards who decimated the Aztecs, not so much with military prowess as with disease—be carrying the thing oneself. Vacations, like everything else, are different now. So when two friends invited me to travel—one to Peru, one to a beach—I viewed the choice in a new way. The guidebooks from the library made Peru sound like a spawning ground for hepatitis, dysentery, tropical disease. ("You're either an intrepid traveler or you're not," said the British friend going there). Saint Thomas was safe—too safe, perhaps— and answered that longing the friend felt when he said, "There must be a beach at the end of this." Perhaps there's a beach in the middle of it, I thought, as the last small plane droned over Vieques, Culebra, and nameless cays in a sea one would compare to jewels (amethysts, aquamarines) if it hadn't been already. Americans now come down to these islands the way they take aspirin—thanks to advertising agencies—and for the same reason: to recover their health. The passengers in the airport in Charlotte Amalie, in fact, confirmed my suspicions about this particular trip—that it would be like not leaving the United States at all. When the taxi took us from the airport into Charlotte Amalie, the capital of the U.S. Virgin Islands seemed an odd cross between Bedford-Stuyvesant (Brooklyn) and New Hope (Pennsylvania)—busy, crowded, booming, you enter it on a four-lane highway past traffic lights, a Grand Union, a Kentucky Fried Chicken, and three or four Love Boats tied up at the dock so their passengers can search for bargains in crystal, French perfume, and liquor ashore. On a long, lovely flight of stone steps we climbed to reach our guesthouse, I could see bougainvillea, oleander, and a pair of men rolling joints a few feet from the side door of a cathedral in which a small group of parishioners was celebrating Mass.

When we got to the hotel, a cat was curled around the railing of the terrace high above the harbor—a calico cat suspended above the bougainvillea, and church bells, and hummingbirds nosing yellow waxy flowers as big as goblets. The cat was sleepy, fat, and content. I was not. I was demented; I insisted we go swimming before the sun had set, so my friend and I changed into bathing suits and hopped a bus that went to the beach nearest town, just beyond the airport, Brewer's Bay. Riding the bus was the perfect baptism: poking in and out of suburban roads, dropping people home after work, the wind through the open windows, the statues on the bus dashboard, the pink shutters on the chartreuse houses were all laid-back and reassuring. There were planes taking off and landing just beyond Brewer's Bay, but they didn't matter—its scimitar of white sand, palm trees, clear water, view of distant crags were, even in a warm rain, the beach one had seen in the travel brochures for years. And the next morning we took the boat from Charlotte Amalie to the island with the most photographed, the most gorgeous, beaches of all—Saint John. The ferries that take you from Saint Thomas to Saint

John look, but exactly, like the blue-and-white ferries that took us from Sayville to Fire Island in the seventies. I thought, *Perhaps they are the same boats, in retirement.* In fact the Virgin Islands had always been one of the places certain people from Fire Island used to go after the water was turned off in the Pines in autumn. Yet we saw no homosexuals. We were surrounded by numerous young heterosexual couples whose inability to sit together without touching, holding, entwining their legs together suggested this was honeymoon. It was all right that there were no other homosexuals—that, too, reflects the plague—I had a friend with whom I liked to travel. And once on Saint John, we took a taxi to Trunk Bay—one of the ten most beautiful beaches in the world, according to *National Geographic*—and we found lots of people. Paperback novels by Danielle Steel anchored the towels while kids on vacation from prep school tossed Frisbees at the water's edge. We were in Connecticut—so we fled the sun and hiked one of the trails cut through the national park that, courtesy of the Rockefellers (who donated the land—otherwise Saint John would be as suburban as Saint Thomas), covers most of the island.

You can be quite alone in the woods on Saint John— everyone else is on the beach—and walking down a densely wooded slope to a cove three miles away, the only thing to remind you that you are not on Treasure Island is the occasional sign placed at the base of a tree identifying the species' origin, history, and uses. The sun winks above the canopy of glossy, exotic leaves, and the dry riverbed beside you is full of vines—the kind Tarzan swings on—and as you walk to a beach you have never seen before, the coast, glimpsed from a break in the forest, is marked by a cluster of coconut palms rising above a swatch of brilliant turquoise sea. When you get there, you find an abandoned stone house on which lizards and bougainvillea are dozing

in the sun, and, down below in a cove, a slender sailboat
from which travelers are setting out in an inflated orange
raft to snorkel along a cliff. It is perfect. It is *Swept Away*.
People go to sunny islands to unwind, to be recharged, as
if the touch of hot cement against one's back, the stillness
of a lizard on a stone, the light of sun on water, will make
us well again. A friend of mine used to go to a Dutchman
in the East Village for a Shiatsu massage when he was sick;
the only way he could be caressed in those days, in the
sense of hands upon the body. Heat upon the body is what
this empty terrace above this sun-bleached cove gives the
tired traveler now: a whole morning, and half an afternoon, of sunlight, stored up in the smooth stone. Going
back it is as if one has been in a trance—something has
been found. We are picked up on the highway by a hearty
young woman from Texas who manages a delicatessen in
Charlotte Amalie and a man who has worked on sailboats
till now and never come ashore. "This has been the best
day of my life," she exults. ("This isn't paradise," counters
her boyfriend. It is all subjective, finally.) We stop for a
drink in a bar perched above Coral Bay and watch a woman
chase a donkey running away from a dog. Later they leave
us at the top of another small peak so we can walk down
a trail to swim at sunset in yet another of the world's Ten
Most Beautiful Beaches: Cinnamon Bay. (This one truly
is.) The beach is deserted, the islands on the horizon are
turning dark while the sky behind turns paler and paler
gold. The town on Saint John—Cruz Bay—is so quiet, so
dark when we finally get back, that after a beer and a conch
fritter, we sit invisible on a bench in the square and watch
people come and go.

Nothing is indigenous to these islands—neither the mango
tree, which comes from Asia, nor the ancestors of the current inhabitants, who caused the Arawak Indians to disappear. The black people seem native to the islands only

because one associates blacks with hot climates. But there are almost as many whites, who have settled here because they like island life. The mix of people who come ashore in Cruz Bay is no less various than the clouds of tropical fish I've been ogling today: sophomores on spring break from Andover talking to Rastafarian fishermen, white-haired retirees to young New Wave couples in backpacks. There are countless Absolute Blondes, on the spectrum of the Three Johns: O'Hara, Cheever, and Updike. Much later two drunken servicemen go around kicking garbage cans —perhaps it's not rowdy enough for them here—but that is the sole incident. Otherwise it is so serene, so dark, I rise with a yawn, say I'm going back to the room we've rented from a woman named Hulga Sewer up the street, and discover as I pass a hardware store with a clock that it is nine-thirty. There is no fighting it. My friend remains to follow the two homosexuals he has spotted, one of them *his type*. In the room I take a last rueful look at that erotic decor—tiled floors, ceiling fans, the glow of one's Jockey shorts in the dark—that years ago might have demanded a partner, or left one morose without one—and in the morning awake to the shrill, high bird song of children singing across the street in a day-care center. We buy oranges in a blue grocery and walk to the harbor to join a snorkeling excursion we stayed overnight to take. The other passengers on the little boat that takes us out of the harbor to a nearby cay are WASPs—the public-TV and museum crowd. One lady over seventy jumps into the water in a wet suit. (Oh, to reach seventy.) Our crew is a young blond woman from Ohio we met in the bar the previous evening—sitting alone with her drink and a smile hovering on the edge of her lips waiting for a chance to use it. The captain is a wiry blond with glasses in faded jeans and T-shirt who barks a stern, no-nonsense introduction, takes us to the cay offshore, and anchors above the spot he says is best. He is right; a few feet off this tiny spine of land with its scrub trees and shell-strewn beach is a spectacular setting of the reef.

One forgets the obsessions of the plague best in the sky or underwater: If Middle Earth is too much with us, go above or below it. The latter is simpler and so, with a flick of our flippers, we set out mindlessly over the ravines and outcroppings of coral, the strange, ghostly, silent, and slightly melancholy region of sea and sand. The first time I come upon a dense cloud of fish, I pop up out of the water to tell the others—but when I do, I cannot even see the snorkels, and realize this is not *de rigueur*. It is, once in the (surprisingly) cool water, a solitary business—each person goes his own way, silent and uncommunicative. The ideal of snorkeling is the feeling one is all alone but not quite forgotten (the feeling, perhaps, of *la peste*). The reef beneath is awesome: great staghorn and elkhorn and brain corals, covered with tiny metallic clusters of fish feeding on organisms that coat their spines. The shafts of light falling from the surface of the sea here illumine an even deeper cave where the edge of the reef plunges at a rakish angle to the sea floor to a soft white clearing of sand amid the rock—all scary at first because the senses are altered, the only sound the husky, dry rasp of one's breath in the snorkel; the sound of someone on a respirator. The light is dimmer than that above the sea, and everything is shadowy and slow. This is about as far away from the hideous world we now live in as it is possible to be. An hour easily passes here on the border between fear and wonder—and when we rejoin the mother ship, our captain takes us to yet another cay, whose reef is far more shallow, more beautiful, more popular with fish (three traits linked even here), so that by the time we putter back into the harbor, my friend and I decide to stay another night. The pre-Easter lull means there is a spare tent at the campground on

Cinnamon Bay—generally one has to reserve weeks, or months, in advance—and, happy in a way I never was a Boy Scout, I take the fresh linen they give me and walk to our tent in a clearing in the jungle. This *is* the most beautiful beach of all—two beaches, in fact, which form a point opposite an island whose reef one can swim to, and whose rocky outcrop is only the nearest of several islands on the horizon, which, along with the forest, the palms, the pellucid water, make this bay nonpareil. In a camp at night, however, I've forgotten there is nothing to do but read, play cards and parlor games—but when we walk down to the open-air dining room, we find among the people playing Trivial Pursuit and reading the Bible (the two themes of American culture) two pairs of male lovers—from San Francisco and Portland—who travel together each year and have been at Cinnamon Bay all week. We play Hearts with them. We drink rum. It is so much fun (the fun of preplague), the married man who has struck up a friendship with the lovers from San Francisco watches us from the table he shares nearby with his wife. He says—seeing us drink rum—"Bet there'll be lots of shiny asses on the beach tonight!"

He is right. What he remembers wistfully from fraternity days we re-create on the beach later on—the air so bright, the water so clear, you can see every hair on your body when you look down, swimming along the shore. *This* is the Definitive Swim, I think for the fifth time. All that we went through to find this place—the bustle and deadends—is irrelevant in this splendor. Somewhere there *is* an island of your dreams. I'm happy as the cat in Charlotte Amalie—even if the old, giddy excitement that drenched forests and beaches and narrow paths in the dark wood from Cape Cod to Fire Island to Land's End is faint now —it's but remembered music, a dance from the past. The lovers are down the beach, dark figurines in the blazing moonlight, asking my friend what our "relationship" is; but the reality is this—I keep diving down to the soft sand bottom, revolving over and over again under the moonlight, watching the gin-clear water slip over my stomach and chest, swimming up and down the shore. The swimmer is trying, in some peculiar way, to swim enough in this gorgeous sea to cleanse himself—though he knows the thing that must be cleansed floats in an interior sea, and no amount of seawater slipping over the skin can wash it away. I have arrived in these islands a decade after Eddie came down here on a passenger ship filled entirely with homosexuals—and went to all of the reefs and islands (Virgin Gorda, the Baths, Buck Island) which surround this island and lure the traveler on to even less populated, more pristine lagoons. This cruise now seems in retrospect as fairy-tale as the ship in *Amarcord*. How could the passengers have known what the future held!

That the present—their future—has gaps in it, strange silences, and missing people; holes in the city, ghosts on the dance floor, people whose shriek, whose laughter, whose reactions, like Eddie's, one sometimes recalls whenever one hears a song or sees a face or comes down to swim in a sea like this one. If we've had fun with a friend, then all the fun we will have in the world he's been subtracted from requires a little wine spilled from the goblet for the gods —an "Eddie would have loved this," or "Eddie should be here now." The fact that people die does not mean we stop talking to them. It may mean we start talking to them. Especially when the people who have been left behind feel guilty about the fact; baffled by the accident of their own survival. *Why me?* ask the dying. *Why me?* ask the living. And what to do with health that seems as gratuitous as illness? The longer one lives, the more arbitrary, fragile, magical the world—with its islands and starry nights— seems; and, at the same time, the more brutal and unappeasable its facts: the virus, the falling brick. "What's the point in going on?" someone, discouraged by the death of yet another lover, asked my friend. "To bear witness," he replied. And to live. *You must be happy,* said the doctor, *anyway you can.* The paradox of the plague has been how gallant, calm, brave, witty certain people with AIDS seem, in contrast to those who only fear they'll get it. It's the fearful who turn sentimental about everything. Perhaps I would have outgrown Eddie had he not died at the age of forty. Perhaps he would have left New York—and dwindled into someone who sends you postcards over the years from foreign places. It is hard to imagine Eddie's enthusiasm—which turned even his illness, and treatments, into that adventure he confided each afternoon on the phone—fading; like the woman who jumped overboard at the age of seventy in face mask and flippers, he would have gone on discovering things to look at, and do. He would have seen all the islands, eventually: a not-unworthy goal. The world never seems so miraculously beautiful, so obviously a gift, as when we learn we will lose it. Eddie died early, before he could know how widespread the plague would be; when he got the news from his dentist that there were tumors on his gums, he was planning to go around the world. "Aren't you glad you were born in the U.S.?" he said to me one evening as he was dressing to go to work at a nightclub near Union Square. "I'm so happy I was born in the United States with a big, fat dick, and not on some garbage mound in Egypt!"

It was one of those crazy remarks he made from time to time to which there was no conventional response; though at the moment I remembered a professor in college who used to call this idea *moral luck.* Now it seems the garbage mound—in Zaire, if not Egypt—got him anyway. Sex plus jumbo jets; from the joys of liberation to the horrors of leprosy in one short decade. What all the facts and all the accounts of AIDS have somehow failed to deal with is the suffering; and the lack of meaning. I suspect Eddie—had this never happened—would be in Australia now—swimming in another sea; a man who, were he a statue in a park, would have a single inscription on its base: *Enjoy.*